A
VOYAGE
ROUND THE WORLD
IN THE YEARS
1785, 1786, 1787, AND 1788.

Captain Portlock and Dixon Purchaseing Skins of the Indians.

A VOYAGE ROUND THE WORLD

IN THE YEARS
1785, 1786, 1787, AND 1788.
PERFORMED IN THE KING GEORGE, COMMANDED BY CAPTAIN PORTLOCK; AND THE QUEEN CHARLOTTE, COMMANDED BY CAPTAIN DIXON;

BY

C.L.,

SHIP'S SURGEON ABOARD THE QUEEN CHARLOTTE

YE GALLEON PRESS
Fairfield, Washington

F
851.5
.C2
1984

Library of Congress Cataloging in Publication Data

C.L.
    A voyage round the world in the years 1785, 1786, 1787 and 1788.

    Reprint. Originally printed: London : R. Randal, 1789.   1. Northwest coast of America — Description and travel. 2. Voyages around the world. 3. C.L. I. Title.
F851.5.C2   1984   910.4′1   84-11975
ISBN 0-87770-325-6

PENROSE MEMORIAL LIBRARY
WHITMAN COLLEGE
WALLA WALLA, WASHINGTON 99362

INTRODUCTION

C.L., the author of this work, has remained anonymous. However, on comparing the text of his description of the voyage with those of [Beresford]-Dixon and Captain Portlock, all three of whom published their accounts in London in 1789, it becomes apparent that C.L. was on board the Queen Charlotte *together with Beresford. His description of the voyage follows closely that of Beresford, and at times the phraseology is almost identical. Further investigation has disclosed that there was a surgeon on board the* Queen Charlotte *whose name was given by Beresford as Lauder, although his first initial is not mentioned. He was a young Scot, 22 years old, who befriended Beresford and even shared his own bunk with him at the start of the voyage, until other accommodations were found for Beresford. The British Museum has very kindly done some research on the Scottish family of Lauder and traced a surgeon named Colin Lauder listed in medical directories during the period of 1772-1809 and in James Young's* Notes *on historical references to the Scottish family of Lauder (1884). He was most probably the anonymous writer. The only problem is the fact that Portlock in his* Voyage round the world *(see No. 42), lists* Queen Charlotte's *surgeon as* William *Lauder. Perhaps his full name was William Colin Lauder. Summing up, the assumption that C.L. was William Colin Lauder is not unreasonable. In view of his friendship with Beresford, he undoubtedly had access to Beresford's notes of the voyage and wrote his own work with these in mind. His text incidentally is completely different from that of Portlock, for obvious reasons, including the fact that the* King George *and the* Queen Charlotte *parted ways on the high seas more than once.*

It should be noted here that a verbatim reprint of C.L.'s account appeared in a Dublin edition the same year, 1789, small octavo (printed by and for J. Whitworth, No. 14 Exchange Street). The t.p. is identical with C.L.'s London edition, except for the imprint as mentioned above, and a different frontispiece. The one in the Dublin edition represents a family of Patagonians "lately discovered," of gigantic height as compared with the British seaman (an officer?) standing beside them, who is represented as being about half the height of the Patagonians.

Both the London and the Dublin editions of C.L.'s text are shorter and, on the whole, considerably inferior to the [Beresford]-Dixon text, as well as much less attractive in format and printing quality. They also lack the plates found in the [Beresford]-Dixon relation. Nevertheless, from the bibliographical point of view, C.L.'s work seems to be quite rare, as there are only 3 known copies of the London edition in the United States—those of Yale University and the New York Public Library, the latter having 2 copies. The British Museum does not seem to have it.

Introduction taken from *Bibliography of Books on Alaska Published Before 1868*, by Valerian Lada-Mocarski, pp. 164-166. Yale University Press, pub., New Haven, Connecticut, 1969. Reprinted courtesy of Yale University Press.

SOME NOTES

The Voyage Round the World in the Years 1785, 1786, 1787 and 1788 *by William Colin Lauder (??) and presumably the rarest book pertaining to the Northwest Coast of America, was printed in London in 1789, and also in Dublin the same year. I believe that a few more original copies are held by U.S. libraries than those listed in Lada-Mocaski . . .a very valuable reference work. I list the following:*

> *New York Public Library, two copies*
> *The Bancroft Library, Berkeley, Califorma, two copies, with variant title pages, with and without the price of three shillings.*
> *John Carter Brown Library, Providence, Rhode Island*
> *The Beinecke Library, Yale University, New Haven, Connecticut*

It is possible that some copies might be held by collectors of Americana.

A microfilm copy is held by the University of Utah in Salt Lake City.

The University of Pennsylvania, Philadelphia according to the Library of Congress The National Union Catalog Pre-1956 Imprints *is listed as holding a copy of the 1789 Dublin edition, if so, this could be the only such copy in the U.S.*

I have no knowledge of any printings of this title between 1789 and the Ye Galleon title of 1985.

Glen Adams

publisher

NOTES

Should the mildly erratic pagination of this book bother sensitive readers the publisher explains that the decision was to leave the old 1790 page numbers. The London printer had two page 92's, one facing page 91 and one facing page 93. Also the page numbers take an unusual step from page 144 to page 150 . . .illustrating something I have long suspected, that eighteenth century book printers had their moments of weakness . . .as do twentieth century bookprinters. The 1790 edition of course had no index, common for books of the day. An index was added to the Ye Galleon edition for the convenience of present day readers . . .many of whom believe firmly in indexes.

A VOYAGE ROUND THE WORLD,

IN THE YEARS

1785, 1786, 1787, AND 1788.

PERFORMED IN THE KING GEORGE,

COMMANDED BY CAPTAIN PORTLOCK;

AND THE QUEEN CHARLOTTE,

COMMANDED BY CAPTAIN DIXON;

Under the Direction of the Incorporated Society for
THE ADVANCEMENT OF THE FUR TRADE.

LONDON:

Printed for R. RANDAL, No. 1, Shoe-lane, Fleetstreet,
and sold by all Booksellers in Town and Country.

M DCC LXXXIX.
[PRICE THREE SHILLINGS.]

CONTENTS.

CHAP I.

REASONS for undertaking the voyage—Account of the ships, and their destination—Sail from the river—arrive at Gravesend—cast anchor near Margate—arrive off Deal—anchor at Spithead—proceed to Guernsey—see Porto Santo, and Madeira. Arrive at Saint Jago—Description of it.   1

CHAP. II.

Leave St. Jago—Account of crossing the Line—Continuation of the voyage from St. Jago to Falkland's Islands—Our arrival there—Amusements and employments—Some account of their productions—birds, fish, &c.—Proceed towards Cape Horn—Anchor in Karakkakooa Bay.   10

CHAP III.

Disappointed in procuring water at Owhyhee—proceed to Whahoo—purchase water there—Proceed to Oneehow—obtain a plentiful supply of yams—Passage to Cook's River—meet with some Russian adventurers—anchor in Coal-Harbour.   20

CHAP. IV.

Leave Coal-Harbour—Proceed up Cook's River—Purchase variety of skins from the natives of the coasts.   28

CHAP V.

Account of the furs collected in Cook's River—Proceed for the Sandwich Islands—A fiery meteor observed—Description of part of the coast of Owhyhee.   37

CHAP. VI.

Visited by Teereteera, king of Whahoo—The natives attempt to steal the whale-boat.—A priest comes on board—his method of taking the ava.—Account of an human sacrifice.—The injustice of Teereteera.—Piapia resolves to come to England.—Depart from Atoui.   46

CHAP. VII.

Proceed to Wymoa-Bay, Atoui—Are visited by Abbenoue and his son—The king comes on board—Several officers of the ship take a little tour up the country—Several of the officers entertained by Abbenoue.   57

CHAP. VIII.

Arrive at Wymoa Bay, Atoui—find the inhabitants toboo-

CONTENTS.

ed.—*Attempt to make Owhyhee—Steer for the American coast.—Arrive at Prince William's Sound.—Captain Dixon takes an excursion in a whale-boat.—Find the Nootka, Capt. Meares, in a creek.*   64

CHAP IX.
Plan of separation agreed on—A chief and his people bring a letter—they commit several thefts on board—Narrow escape of a fishing party—Discover an excellent harbour, which we named Port Mulgrave—Manners and customs of the inhabitants—Method of disposing of their dead.   80

CHAP. X.
Quit Port Mulgrave—Anchor in Norfolk Sound—Various proceedings there—Persons, manners, and customs of the inhabitants of Norfolk Sound.   91

CHAP. XI.
Leave Norfolk Sound—Anchor in Port Banks—Reasons for quitting it—Find a great number of Indians, who traffic largely with us—Several other parties of Indians trade with us.—Arrive off Queen Charlotte's Islands.   97

CHAP. XII.
Obervations on Queen Charlotte's Islands—Meet two vessels, called the Prince of Wales, and the Princess Royal, from London—Persons, manners, and customs of the inhabitants—Dress—Manufactures.   110

CHAP. XIII.
Teereteere comes on board to take leave—Proceed to Atoui.—Liberal behaviour of the king and chiefs.—Manners and customs of the Sandwich Islanders.   120

CHAP XIV.
Leave Atoui - Proceed for China—Pass the Islands of Tinian, Aguigan, and Saypan—Anchor in Macao Roads—Leave Macao—Arrive at Wampo—Difficulties occasioned by the supercargoes there.   129

CHAP XV.
Leave Wampo.—Anchor in the Roads of North Island.—dangerous storm.—proceed to St. Helena—procure water there, and some fresh beef.—Arrive off Dover.   137

PREFACE.

THAT great circumnavigator, Captain Cook, whose memory will be ever revered, has not only increased the stock of Geographical knowledge beyond any man who has preceded him; but, by his discoveries, has opened a wide field for Commerce, established an intercourse between the unlettered Indian and the polished European, and pointed out a source of wealth to the adventurous merchant.

From his indefatigable labours, and superior nautical abilities, civilization will probably be introduced among the most barbarous savages, science rear her head in the uncultivated desert, and posterity in general derive advantages, which would have been unthought of and unknown, had not Heaven favoured the admiring world with so great a navigator, with such a friend to society.

Induced by the discoveries made in his last voyage to the Pacific Ocean, and particularly by the lucrative prospect which he had pointed out

PREFACE.

out for the advancement of the fur trade; many have since visited those regions, which were before unexplored by the European.

Enterprising merchants, from different nations, have availed themselves of his labours and ingenuity; and a society of Gentlemen in England, incorporated by charter, purchased two ships for the sole purpose of extending that invaluable branch of commerce. Messieurs Portlock and Dixon were appointed commanders of those ships, and I had the honour to attend them in their expedition; the particulars of which are faithfully related in the following pages.

C. L.

A VOYAGE ROUND THE WORLD.

CHAP. I.

Reasons for undertaking the voyage—Account of the ships, and their destination—Sail from the river—arrive at Gravesend—cast anchor near Margate—arrive off Deal—anchor at Spithead—proceed to Guernsey—see Porto Santo, and Madeira. Arrive at Saint Jago—Description of it.

OUR vessels being perfectly equipped for a voyage round the world, with a view to establish a valuable fur trade on the American coast, and to dispose of our commodity to advantage at China; we weighed anchor on the 29th of August 1785 at nine o'clock in the morning, and stood for Gravesend. Of our two ships, the larger was called the King George, and commanded by Captain Portlock, who was also commander in chief for the voyage; the smaller, named the Queen Charlotte, was commanded by Captain Dixon. The former veffel had about fixty on board, and the latter little more than half that number.

The wind and tide proving favourable, we came to anchor at Gravefend about two o'clock in the afternoon. Here a difficulty arofe, which I was apprehenfive would have retarded our voyage. The articles of agreement being read to the fhips' crews, they refufed to fign them without an advance upon the ufual wages. But Captain Portlock expoftulated with them on the impropriety of their demand, and they chearfully complied with the terms which were propofed.

On the 30th the men were paid their wages, and a month's falary in advance, which they expended in purchafing neceffaries of the flop boats, which always attend upon thefe occafions. At eleven o'clock we weighed anchor and ftood for the Downs, and caft anchor near Margate about eight the fame evening. We again weighed the next morning, and brought to abreaft of Deal in the afternoon; where, on account of contrary winds, we continued till the morning of the fecond of September,

ber, when a favourable breeze sprung up, and we made sail.

We proceeded, without much variety, till the fifth, when a heavy gale sprung up, and our vessel became the sport of the winds and waves: disorder and confusion became general by the creaking of the ship's timbers, the noise and bustle of the seamen, and the outrageous howlings of the wind. But, when the evening advanced, the storm abated, though the billows rolled mountains high. In the morning the angry waves recovered their serenity, and we came to anchor at Spithead on the evening of the 8th of September.

Here we beheld the masts of the Royal George, in which Admiral Kempenfeldt among 15 persons of various descriptions, found a watery grave. At this place we took in live stock and other necessaries.

In the morning of the 16th of September we left Spithead, and passed by St. Helen's about eleven; but were induced, by the wind and weather, to return and anchor in St. Helen's road in the evening. On the 17th, at seven in the evening, we made sail, the weather being moderate and the winds variable till the 19th; on the

evening

evening of which we were at anchor with a kedge; and a cutter, which was to convey some ladies we had on board to Guernsey on a party of pleasure, was moored to our stern with a strong rope. With the rapidity of the tide, for we had not then much wind, the rope broke, and the cutter run adrift; and we also lost the flake of our anchor.

In the forenoon of the 20th, we saw what are called the Caskets; a cluster of rocks often fatal to mariners. Being quite becalmed, our vessel became unmanageable, and, in the evening, we were not above a mile from them. Though we had soundings in twenty fathom water, the bottom consisted only of sharp rocks, so that there was no probability of an anchor being of any service to us. Happily, however, the tide turned about nine o'clock, and, for that time, removed our apprehensions of danger.

About noon on the 21st, being near the harbour of Guernsey, our owners brought a pilot on board to take us in, and we anchored in Guernsey road about seven o'clock in the evening. The trade of this place is chiefly of the contraband kind, which is carried on extensively with France, Spain, and Portugal. Brandy, wines, &c. they deal in to a confiderable amount, but tea is no longer a lucrative article in clandeftine dealings. The women here are naturally far from handfome, but, by a judicious ufe of paint, fome of them appear to have pretty good complexions.

Here we took feveral articles from the Royal George on board the Queen Charlotte, and procured a ftock of liquor. On the 26th we weighed, and made fail; and, on the 27th, faw feveral iflands at the diftance of about feven leagues.

About eleven in the morning on the 2d of October, fomething appeared at a diftance floating on the water: the curiofity of every one was excited. Fearlefs of the attacks of fharks, two of the men prevailed upon Captain Dixon to fuffer them to plunge into the fea. The expected prize was found to be a large cafk, covered with barnacles, a well-known fhell-fifh. It was hoifted on board, after having probably remained a long time in the water, the fifh having almoft eaten holes through the cafk, and could with difficulty be removed. On examination we found ourfelves rewarded with a hogfhead of claret; but, though the acquifition might be agreeable to us, we could not avoid heaving a figh for

the

the situation of those, who found it expedient to part with any thing so valuable.

Nothing remarkable occurred till the 13th, when early in the morning Porto Santo appeared, at the distance of about seven leagues, and Madeira somewhat nearer. On the 16th we saw Palma and Ferro, two of the Canary Islands, and Bonavista on the 24th. At noon on the same day, we anchored in Port Praya Bay, St. Jago.

The island of St. Jago is about one hundred miles in circuit, and the climate very hot; the easterly winds blowing from the sandy deserts of Africa, contributing to augment the heat. Here we intended to procure water, fresh provisions, and other necessaries. The reception we met with from the commander of the fort, was far from being flattering to us; but a trifling present purchased his civility, and we were permitted to water our ships: more was not in his power to grant, other necessaries being only to be procured of a Portuguese merchant, who resided at some distance.

The two captains, accompanied by some of the officers, waited on this merchant, who received them with much civility and politeness,

politeness, and entertained them with excellent Madeira and fruits. A guinea was paid for each vessel, as a kind of port charge; and the captains were required to enter their names in a book provided for that purpose, as well as mention from whence they came, and the particulars of their destination.

Captain Portlock agreed to purchase some beef and other articles from this gentleman; but was informed by an old negro, who spoke a little broken English, that they might be furnished with whatever they wanted, on cheaper terms, by the country people. At Praya we found a kind of market, attended by persons from various parts of the island, with sheep, hogs, goats, fowls, pine-apples, oranges, and other excellent fruits, cocoa-nuts, bananas, &c. The merchant indeed was the only person who could furnish us with beef, the poverty of the common inhabitants not permitting them to deal in articles of that magnitude and price, though the bullocks are much smaller than those which are produced in Wales or Scotland.

Toys and old cloaths were more coveted by these people than cash, which was a

fortu-

fortunate circumstance, English coin not being current in this place. But we were obliged to advance some money, which we procured by exchanging guineas for dollars with the merchant, on very disadvantageous terms.

During our continuance in this island, three ships arrived from London, and a brig from America. The American came to purchase horses or cattle; but not being able to procure any, he departed in a few hours. The London vessels are employed in the southern whale fishery.

The fort and castle here make a very insignificant appearance, though commanded by a captain, and having a small garrison of soldiers. On a plain behind the fortress, stands the town of Praya, consisting of about sixty huts at a considerable distance from each other, and forming a kind of square, in which the market is held. These habitations are composed of stone, without any cement, and are the most miserable residences that can be conceived. Beds are but little known in this island, mats are in general used to repose on. The natives, who are black, act principally as servants to the Portuguese, many of whom are inhabitants of this place. The Roman Catholic

lic religion, with all the bigotry of Portugal, is exercifed here.

From the warmth of the climate, the females here might have been fuppofed to have been amorous; yet neither prefents nor folicitations from our gentlemen, could prevail upon either the natives or the Portuguefe, to gratify their wifhes.

Goats are very plentiful in this ifland, and their milk fupplies the inhabitants with a principal part of their fubfiftence. Befides other methods of ufing it for food, great quantities of it are ufed in making cheefe. Little cloathing is required in fuch a climate, and very little is ufed: the women indeed wear a loofe covering, compofed of cotton, a thin petticoat, and a cap. Their ears and necks are alfo embellifhed with beads, and a crofs is ufually fufpended from the neck. The countenances of the Portuguefe are fallow, wan, and meagre; thofe of the natives have the appearance of health and vigour.

CHAP. II.

Leave St. Jago—Account of crossing the Line—Continuation of the voyage from St. Jago to Falkland's Islands—Our arrival there—Amusements and employments—Some account of their productions—birds, fish, &c.—Proceed towards Cape Horn—Anchor in Karakkakooa Bay.

OUR necessities being in a great measure supplied, a favourable breeze sprung up, and we weighed anchor on the morning of the 29th of October. As we approached the equinoctial line, it became gradually hotter, and, on the 3d of November, the heat was so intense, that it was thought expedient to wash our decks and vessels with vinegar. That task was carefully performed. From the 4th to the 12th of November, there was a succession of squalls, calms, clear and hazy weather, and thunder and lightning. On the 16th we crossed the line, and the usual ceremony of plunging those under water, who had never been to the south of it, was begun; but some of the men appearing to be much enraged at such treatment, the captain gave a double allowance of grog to all hands, which terminated the dispute. The liquor, however, had a pernicious operation upon some of them, who grew so turbulent and unmanageable, that it was found necessary to confine them in irons.

On

On the 24th, vinegar was served out to every man, which was found very salutary with their salt provisions, fish, &c. On the 25th they had unexpectedly a supply of slops, which afforded them much satisfaction, as they apprehended they should not be able to procure a supply of cloaths. Tea and sugar were delivered to them on the 26th, sufficient to furnish them with a breakfast every morning. These were doubly agreeable, as a comfortable addition to our food, and as anti-scorbutics.

Being at length out of the Tropics, on the 6th of December the weather began to be agreeable, accompanied with steady easterly breezes. We had a heavy gale on the 11th, but the weather soon became moderate. The 16th, it being moderate and fine, many spermaceti whales appeared about the ship. We had so heavy a gale of wind on the 21st, that we were obliged to hand our top-sails, and reef our courses, and take every method to keep the vessel dry and in order. Southward of the line, this is the longest day, the sun rising before four o'clock here in December. On the 23d, we saw a seal, and a multitude of fish playing about the ship. The next morning we had a heavy storm of snow and sleet, and we had had heavy gales of wind and squally weather for the three preceding days. About this time we had a goat ſtarved to death with cold, though the utmoſt care had been taken of it. We regretted its loſs, as it had furniſhed us with milk twice a day.

Early on the 25th we had freſh breezes, and tolerably clear weather, but at four o'clock we had a heavy gale of wind. This being Chriſtmas day, it was celebrated as a feſtival, by tumultuous joy and mirth, accompanied with inebriation, occaſioned by drinking grog to the health of abſent friends. For ſeveral ſucceſſive days, we had variety of weather; for, though this is the ſummer in this part of the world (being in latitude 50 deg. 32 min. ſouth) yet the weather, at this time, reſembled that of March in England.

On the 1ſt of January 1786, it was apparent that we were not far from land, from the number of birds that came about us. About four o'clock in the morning we diſcovered land, at the diſtance of nine or ten leagues. At nine we founded in eighty fathom water. In the afternoon we founded again in nearly the ſame depth. In the morning of the 3d, at nine o'clock, we ſaw a rock at about ſix leagues diſtance, which we at firſt ſuppoſed to be a veſſel

under

under sail. We were afterwards informed that this rock is known by the name of the Eddystone. Unwilling to lose sight of the land, we stood in shore, and tacked occasionally. On the 4th, in the morning, we saw two small islands, and continued to stand along shore, supposing we were at no great distance from Port Egmont. At one the next morning, being within a league of the westernmost land, the commodore made a signal to stand off shore. At three we were under sail, and Captain Portlock dispatched his first mate to look out for a harbour.

About eight the mate fired a musket as a signal for danger, and at ten hoisted a flag on an eminence, which was a signal for a harbour: both ships therefore stood in for the sound, and the commodore made a signal for the mate to return, by firing a gun. He soon made his appearance, and acquainted us that he had seen a reef of rocks, which induced him to fire; and further informed us, that the harbour afforded an excellent place for watering. About twelve both ships anchored in Port Egmont.

Our principal object was to water the ships, and to lay in some additional ballast

in

in the Queen Charlotte, having obferved that fhe did not draw a fufficient depth of water. No time was loft in accomplifhing thefe two objects, and on the 14th we had completed our bufinefs entirely. During this fhort fpace, all the people had been on fhore to breathe a little land air; a common practice upon thefe occafions, and thought to be of effential fervice to the health of feamen.

On the 14th an Englifh floop arrived in the harbour, which we were afterwards informed was called the United States, and commanded by a Captain Huffey. She was the property of Mrs. Hayley, widow of alderman Hayley, and fifter to the prefent chamberlain of London.

Our captains, after taking a regular furvey of the port, and making other neceffary refearches, difcovered a birth for the fhips, fuperior to that in which we lay, on the weft fide of the bay: accordingly we anchored there on the morning of the 16th, and prefently congratulated ourfelves on the change we had made, being well fheltered, and not incommoded with any fwell. Port Egmont is fo capacious a harbour, that the whole navy of Great Britain might ride in it.

In

In the morning of the 19th, we weighed anchor and made sail; and at nine in the evening anchored off Carcase Island. On the 20th we made sail, and anchored in West-point harbour about two in the afternoon. We again made sail on the morning of the 21st, and in rounding West Point, the wind poured upon us like a hurricane, and blew for the space of an hour with such astonishing impetuosity, that we could not display a single yard of canvas; but as we gradually got clear of the high land, the wind grew more moderate. At four in the afternoon we anchored in States Bay, Swan Island.

Tho' these islands are generally known by the name of Falkland's, they have also their individual names, as Swan Island, Keppel's Island, &c. The weather, though it was the height of summer here, was cold and winterly, with frequent heavy rain; the winds too were generally westerly. It is worthy of remark, that a tree, or any thing resembling a tree, is not to be found on these islands. Not an insect of any kind was to be seen, though one of our officers was indefatigable in his endeavours to find objects of that kind.

Geese

Geese and ducks were numerous on the beaches, but they were smaller, and in other respects different from those in England. They are tame, and easily taken; but their flesh was so extremely coarse, rank, fishy, and disagreeable, that we could not relish them as food. The Port-Egmont hen, which is a ravenous bird, somewhat resembling a hawk, are very numerous in these islands. The seapie, however, was the only bird we could find, that had not a rank fishy taste.

Very few fish are found here, except mullets, which are excellent, and frequently taken in large quantities. Large beds of muscles and limputs are seen on the beaches, together with many other marine productions, serving as food for geese, penguins, &c. In the morning of the 23d we made sail. The weather was moderate and hazy till the 26th. About eleven o'clock in the morning, we saw Staten's Island, and during the night we had lightning, attended with frequent squalls. In the morning of the 27th we were about five or six miles from the shore of Staten's Island. The weather continued moderate till the 4th of February.

Not knowing when we should come to anchor,

anchor, on the 7th of March our captain put the ship's company to an allowance of water, each man to have two quarts per day. In the evening of the 25th we faw a veffel to the north-weft, which afterwards paffed us almoft within hail. We know not what country fhe came from, but gueffed her to be a Spaniard going to Baldivia. On the 3d of April, a pint of cider per man each day was begun to be ferved out, which was found highly falutary, as the weather was now become intenfely hot and fultry.

The armourer's forge was fixed upon deck on the 5th of April, and he immediately began to fabricate fundry articles for the ufe of the fhip, as well as what are called toes, for our future traffic. Thefe are long flat pieces of iron, fomewhat narrower than a carpenter's plane-iron, and are much valued by the Indians. Our carpenters were employed in making ports for guns, and frames for fwivels; and, on the tenth, two four-pounders, and eight fwivels, were fixed upon the quarter deck. The heat growing ftill more intenfe, every man's allowance of water was increafed to three quarts per day. We caught feveral fharks towards the conclufion of this month; and, though they are but a coarfe rank kind of food, we confidered them as a valuable acquifition, having lived fo long upon falt provifions. We fed on them with fingular pleafure and fatisfaction.

Still the weather continued hot in the extreme, and hardly a breeze of air was to be perceived. From the 1ft to the 3d of May, we faw a great many turtles, whence we were induced to hope that we were not far diftant from a turtle ifland. With much difficulty we caught one of them; but our commodore, aided by his whale boat, caught upwards of half a fcore per day, and furnifhed us with a large fupply.

The fhip's company had enjoyed a good ftate of health, except the captain and the fecond mate; the former having been attacked with illnefs foon after our leaving St. Jago, and the latter having laboured under a complication of diforders: but the fcurvy now began to make a formidable appearance; many of the people being much affected with it, and others in an inferior degree. All our anti-fcorbutics were employed with care and diligence; but we were foon convinced that our endeavours would be ineffectual, without the affiftance of frefh provifions, vegetables, frefh water, and frefh air: we therefore refolved to make

Sandwich

Sandwich Islands with all possible dispatch, and at eight o'clock in the morning of the 14th, we saw Owhyhee, the principle of those islands, bearing west distance about twelve leagues; and at two o'clock on the 26th, was anchored in Karakkakooa Bay, at a distance of about a mile from shore.

CHAP III.

Disappointed in procuring water at Owhyhee—proceed to Whahoo—purchase water there—Proceed to Oneehow—obtain a plentiful supply of yams—Passage to Cook's River—meet with some Russian adventurers—anchor in Coal-Harbour.

SOON after we came to anchor in Karakkakooa Bay, we were surrounded with canoes; and vast numbers of the inhabitants of Owhyhee, of both sexes, swam about us in the water. Curiosity only induced many of them to visit us; but others brought hogs, plaintains, sweet potatoes, bread-fruit, and various other commodities to sell or barter. For these articles we exchanged nails, toes, fish-hooks, toys, and other trifling articles.

Intending to perform our necessary business with all imaginable dispatch, we began to prepare for watering; but Captain Dixon first visited the King George, where he received information that the inhabitants meant to become troublesome, and had absolutely tabooed the watering place. Those who have read the voyages of Captain Cook, need not be informed that the ceremony of tabooing is performed by the priests, by sticking small wands, tipped with a tuft of white hair, round any spot from which they mean

mean to exclude the people. Some of our officers were apprehenfive that this mode of proceeding was adopted, from their refentment of the treatment they had received after the death of Captain Cook, who loft his life in this harbour. That, however, was not the cafe: the reafon they affigned for their conduct was, that as all their chiefs were abfent, profecuting a war againft the inhabitants of a neighbouring ifland, they durft not prefume to fuffer ftrangers to come on fhore.

It may be neceffary to remark that the Sandwich Iflands were difcovered by Captain Cook, in his laft voyage to the Pacific Ocean; the principal of which, called Owhyhee, being to the fouthward and eaft, the reft being in a north-weft direction. Thefe obtained the name of Sandwich Iflands, from the Earl of Sandwich being firft Lord of the Admiralty when that voyage was undertaken, and indeed at the time of the difcovery of thofe iflands.

On the 27th of June we made fail, the fhip's company being bufily employed in killing and falting hogs. Canoes followed us with thofe animals, plantains, breadfruit, &c.

At noon on the 31ſt, we ſaw Whahoo, another of the Sandwich iſlands; and on the 1ſt of June, at two in the afternoon, we anchored in a bay at the ſouth ſide of it, at the diſtance of half a league from ſhore. A great number of canoes approached us; but hogs and vegetables were not ſo plentiful as we had found them at Owhyhee.

On the 2d both our captains went in ſearch of a watering place, and accommodations for thoſe who were ill. Good water was ſoon found, but the acceſs to it was difficult, and even dangerous, occaſioned by a reef of rocks extending along the bay. We therefore began to deſpair of procuring water at this iſland; but ſome of our officers having obſerved that moſt of the people in the canoes had calabaſhes full of water; Captain Dixon directed us to purchaſe them, which we did on very moderate terms, principally with nails and buttons.

Thus encouraged, the natives eagerly employed themſelves in fetching water for us, and thought themſelves well paid for their labour with a ſmall nail, for bringing about three gallons in a calabaſh. In this ſingular

singular manner, the veffels were soon furnifhed with an ample fupply of water.

While this bufinefs was tranfacting, the furgeon took his patients on fhore, imagining the land air might be ferviceable to them; but the heat of the weather was fo immoderate, and the inhabitants crowded about them in fuch numbers, that they came on board without having received the leaft benefit. Finding we could not procure a fufficient fupply of hogs and vegetables at Whahoo, it was refolved to proceed to Attoui, another of the Sandwich Iflands; and at four in the afternoon of the 7th, we were near Wymoa-Bay, Attoui, where we propofed to come to anchor: but the wind blowing ftrong in a wrong direction, the commodore propofed ftanding for Oneehow, and anchored in Yam-Bay, Oneehow, in the morning of the 8th.

Here we were plentifully furnifhed with excellent yams, in exchange for our nails and trifles. This place produces but little of any thing elfe, and is very thinly inhabited, compared with fome of the other Sandwich Iflands. Here our fick received confiderable benefit from being taken on fhore, as they could walk about without being incommoded by the inhabitants. Abbenooe,

benooe, the principal chief here, received some trifling presents from Captain Portlock, and seemed much inclined to render us any service. The few hogs that we procured here, were chiefly brought from Attoui.

With an excellent stock of yams, and as many hogs as we could get, we made sail on the 13th of June, about eleven in the morning. On the 3d of July we perceived a piece of wood floating on the water, with several birds on it. We frequently observed large quantities of sea-weed, and a species of birds not unlike Cape-pigeons. On the 16th we saw several sea-parrots and other birds, and several pieces of wood passing by us. At 7 o'clock in the evening we beheld land, at the distance of about seven leagues, which we supposed to be bordering on Cook's River. We were amused, during the evening, with seeing a number of whales playing about the vessel.

We were convinced, on the 18th, that the land we had seen on the 26th, was the barren islands at the entrance of Cook's River. In the afternoon of the 18th, we saw the island St. Hermogenes, and whales in great abundance near the land.

We entered Cook's River in the forenoon

noon of the 19th, and having wind and tide in our favour, kept ſtanding along the eaſtern ſhore. About ſix in the evening we heard the report of a gun, which ſurprized us not a little. Our commodore alſo fired a gun, by way of anſwering this ſignal. The report of the gun we firſt heard proceeded from a bay not far from us, which had the appearance of a good harbour. A boat, however, came from the ſhore to the King George, and intelligence was received that they were Ruſſians who had firſt fired.

In the evening, about eight o'clock, we came to anchor, and were ſoon after attended by four or five canoes, with one man in each. Pleaſed with this promiſing appearance, we made aſſortments of our different articles of trade, expecting great quantities of furs to have been offered us in traffic; but, to our infinite concern, we preſently diſcovered that theſe people belonged to the Ruſſians.

Parties were, however, ſent the next morning to procure wood and water, and our captains went in the whale-boat to the Ruſſian factory, in expectation of obtaining ſome intelligence reſpecting their enterprize on this coaſt. We could only learn

from

from them, that they came in a sloop from Oonalaska, and that those whom we had seen in the canoes were Codiac Indians, which they had brought with them to assist them in trafficking with the natives about Cook's River. Having but a very imperfect knowledge of the Russian language, the captains could only comprehend part of what they said: but they understood that they were upon hostile terms with the natives, and never slept without their arms ready loaded by their side.

The Russians had only a temporary residence here, which they had formed by hauling their boats on shore, placing them in the best order they could, and covering them with skins, to shelter them from the inclemency of the weather: but the principal information we acquired was, that they had not been able to procure many skins, though they had nankeens and Persian silks to barter for them.

We laid in a sufficient stock of wood and water by the 26th, and, during that time, our captains, who were out upon the survey, found a vein of coals; a quantity of which were taken on board. Hence the Bay acquired the name of Coal Harbour.

Captain

Captain Portlock having a feine, it was frequently hauled, and generally with fuccefs; large quantities of excellent falmon were often procured by thefe means, and fhared among our people.

CHAP. IV.

Leave Coal-Harbour—Proceed up Cook's River—Purchase variety of skins from the natives of the coasts.

AMPLY furnished with wood and water, we weighed anchor on the morning of the 26th, and directed our course to the main river, in search of inhabitants, who might probably be possessed of furs. The tide of the river was so extremely rapid, that there was a necessity of coming to anchor every tide, without the aid of a fresh favourable breeze. But this circumstance we did not consider as a matter to be lamented; for, as we had much traffic, our frequent anchoring would be indispensably necessary even on that account.

We proceeded up the river on the 26th and 27th, with variable winds, and moderate weather, hourly in expectation of visits from the different inhabitants on the coasts of the river. None, however, came near us. At noon we beheld the Burning Mountain, from whose summit plenty of smoke issued, but we perceived no fire. About four in the afternoon, we anchored at about the distance of three miles from
a level

a level coaſt, expecting the arrival of plenty of canoes, laden with furs. Towards the evening a ſingle canoe approached us, in which was only one perſon. He produced nothing but a little dried ſalmon, for which we gave him a few beads, and he appeared perfectly ſatisfied.

This man was probably diſpatched to learn our intentions; for, when he perceived that we meant amicably to barter with him, and ſaw the variety of articles we dealt in, he ſeemed extremely well ſatisfied, and, principally by his geſtures, which we perfectly underſtood, informed us that the natives on ſhore would bring us a large quantity of ſkins by the next day's ſun.

In the morning of the 29th, we were approached by canoes of various ſizes; ſome containing fourteen men, ſome only one, and others reſpectively laden with all the intervening numbers. Skins of various ſorts were offered us, ſuch as thoſe of bears, ſea-otters, marmots, racoons, and many others, for which they made choice of toes and blue beads. Toes were an article they much delighted in, one of a middling ſize being thought a valuable conſideration for a large otter's ſkin.

We

We traded fuccefsfully during the greater part of the day; the natives behaved with becoming civility and decorum, and we treated them with refpect and good-nature. A fresh gale ftarting in the evening, we had no vifitors; but as the weather was moderate the next morning, many more canoes came along fide, from whom we purchafed a variety of articles.

The weather continued moderate till the 3d of Auguft, and our friends continued to vifit us with fkins of various defcriptions; but they fignified to us that they then acted as agents for diftant tribes in the interior parts of the country. Excellent frefh falmon were fo plenty, that we bought a large one for a fingle bead. The natives catch them in wears, and feed principally on them during the winter, after having fmoaked and dried them in their huts.

No one came near us on the 4th of Auguft, on account of a ftrong breeze; on the 5th the weather again became moderate, and more dealers came with fkins, but they informed us, that we had pretty well drained the country of thofe articles.

In the afternoon of the 6th, Captain Portlock came aboard us, and propofed

weighing

weighing the next morning. In consequence of which we did weigh, but the weather proving unfavourable, Captain Dixon received a message from the commodore, acquainting him that we should continue where we lay. This was a fortunate circumstance, for a very heavy gale of wind came on in the evening, and continued almost the whole night.

In the morning of the 9th of August, the weather became moderate. The natives had ceased to bring us any valuable furs; nothing was now produced but remnants of dirty skins, which had served as garments to the inhabitants.

Early in the morning of the 10th we made sail, having a moderate breeze. At nine we found it necessary to anchor, the tide setting in strongly for land. At six in the afternoon we weighed and made sail, but, unable to stem the tide, we anchored again about five miles distant from the shore. We weighed at five on the 11th; soon after we saw two Russian boats, with about twenty men in each, steering for the island to the southward. We had no doubt but they were the same people we had seen soon after we had entered Cook's River. We kept standing down the river, and at noon

noon on the 12th, Cape Bede bore eaſt ſoutheaſt; at two the Barren Iſlands bore ſouth ſouth-eaſt. The weather was moderate and pretty fine, and we ſuppoſed the next tide, with a tolerable breeze, would take us clear of the river.

We could not preſume to aſcertain the length of the river, as we went no higher than where we lay at anchor; but its breadth appeared in many places to be about twenty miles.

The natives appear harmleſs and inoffenſive in their manners. Their weapons were bows and arrows, and ſpears, which were uſeful both in hunting and fiſhing; they feed on the fleſh of the various beaſts which are inhabitants of that country, and their ſkins conſtitute their cloathing. The animals here are bears, foxes, wolves, racoons, marmots, ermine, muſquaſh, and others of inferior note.

The natives are well proportioned, and of a middle ſize. They ſeem to have regular features, but their faces are ſo covered with filth, that their genuine complexion cannot poſſibly be diſcerned. Only one woman came to viſit us, and ſhe was treated by thoſe who accompanied her with the

greateſt

greatest civility and respect: She might probably be a person of some dignity among them. Her face was clean, her complexion tolerable, and her features rather agreeable than otherwise.

Early in the morning of the 13th of August, we weighed anchor and stood down the river; and before noon we were clear of Cook's River. Our destination being for Prince William's Sound, we kept standing along the shore; and in the afternoon of the 14th, the weather grew cloudy and hazy. On the 16th we kept standing along the shore at the distance of about two leagues. The land we then saw we supposed to be Montague Island, and came to anchor about four o'clock in the afternoon. In the evening of the 18th, a breeze sprung up, when we weighed anchor, and stood in for the shore.

After a variety of unsuccessful attempts, we gave up all hopes of making Prince William's Sound, and our captains agreed to steer for Cross Sound, thinking it probable that skins might be procured there.

Notwithstanding all our endeavours and conjectures, we found ourselves disappointed in our expectations of falling in with

Cross Sound; the Bay of Islands was therefore thought the most eligible harbour for us to make, which was about ten leagues to the south-east. We had a favourable breeze, and expected speedily to make this harbour; but in the morning of the 10th of September, a heavy gale of wind came on, and continued till the evening, when a flat calm succeeded. About three in the morning of the 11th, a heavier gale ensued than that which we had experienced the preceding day, accompanied with rain, which continued till two in the afternoon on the 13th; when the weather became moderate and clear. After this gale we found ourselves about ten leagues from Cape Edgecombe.

Every thing proving contrary to our wishes, and even our expectations, we no longer entertained hopes of making the Bay Islands, but determined to steer for St. George's Sound. Still, however, we intended to keep with the coast, thinking it possible that we might accidentally meet with a harbour. At noon on the 18th, being then steering east, we saw land right a-head, and stood directly for it. At seven o'clock we were well in with land; but seeing no harbour nor inhabitants, we stood to the southward.

Early

Early in the morning of the 26th of September, a moſt vio'ent ſtorm of thunder and lightning came on, accompanied with a heavy rain. The claps of thunder were loud and tremendous beyond conception; and the lightning was ſo aſtoniſhingly fierce, that the people upon deck were for a long time blinded; every flaſh was attended with a ſtrong ſulphureous ſmell.

About five in the morning of the 27th, we made ſail, and ſtood for the harbour at ſix o'clock in the evening; the entrance into Nootka Sound bore north. At five in the morning of the 28th, we again bore up to the Sound; but finding it impoſſible to make the harbour, having had ſome light airs and a heavy ſwell to contend with, we hauled to the ſouthward. At ſix o'clock in the evening, the commodore informed us that it was his intention to quit the coaſt, and proceed for Sandwich Iſlands, at the ſame time directing us to ſteer ſouth ſouth-weſt. In the morning of the 29th, a breeze ſprung up from the weſtward, which enabled us to ſhape our courſe according to the freſh inſtructions we had received. Before night we loſt ſight of the coaſt, and all our hopes of making King George's Sound were loſt for the ſeaſon.

We were remarkably unsuccessful in our endeavours to gain a second harbour on this inhospitable coast. Our disappointment at Cross Sound and Bay Islands proceeded chiefly from wrong informations; and our not making Prince William's, or Nootka Sound, can only be attributed to unfavourable winds and weather.

CHAP V.

Account of the furs collected in Cook's River—Proceed for the Sandwich Islands—A fiery meteor observed—Description of part of the coast of Owhyhee.

DURING the short time we were in Cook's River, we collected about sixty otter-skins of the first quality, and nearly the same number of an inferior kind. We also filled three puncheons with the skins of foxes, racoons, marmots, and other animals. The success of our commodore, in this particular, was, I believe, equivalent to our own.

We experienced, on the 4th of October, some heavy squalls, and close foggy weather. During the night of the seventh, a strong gale blew from the westward; but it grew moderate in the morning of the 8th. In the evening of the 11th, a fiery meteor was seen about the ship, which did not a little alarm our seamen, who, though they have spirit to attack any real danger, are often superstitiously terrified with imaginary evils. What tended to convince them that this phænomenon portended mischief was, that, during the night, we had a heavy gale of wind from the southward, accompanied with much rain. On the 12th,

12th, about nine in the morning, the weather grew moderate, and blew a fresh breeze.

From the 14th to the 24th, nothing particular occurred, excepting that we caught three large sharks on the first of those days, which were very acceptable, the oil of them being found essentially useful for different purposes about the ship.

Some birds appeared about the vessel on the 25th, some of which were so very tame that they might have been caught by the hand, without much difficulty. Some of our officers were of opinion that they were the striated sand-piper, described by Pennant.

The weather was variable, but tolerably fine, from the 25th of October to the 7th of November. On the 8th it was immoderately sultry, and lightning flew in almost every direction. It continued thus on the 9th, in the evening of which it increased to a very alarming degree. A violent gust of wind arose in the morning of the 10th, attended by a heavy rain. It was not, however, of long duration, for it grew moderate in the space of an hour and an half,

and

and we then experienced a cool and temperate air.

On the 9th we caught two dolphins, and on the 12th a shark: in the belly of the latter, a fowl was found, and part of a turtle; it was therefore a natural conjecture that we could not be at any great distance from land. We were indeed pretty certain that Atoui was under our lee.

Sand-pipers, in great abundance, flew about us in the evening. At two o'clock in the afternoon on the 13th, we found ourselves well to winward of Owhyhee, one of the Sandwich Islands which we intended to touch at; we therefore steered more to westward. On the 11th we caught several sharks, in one of which a whole turtle was found. In the afternoon of the 15th, we saw high land, about the distance of ten leagues; we congratulated each other upon this circumstance, as it was known to be Monakeah, a mountain on the island of Owhyhee. Its summit was then covered with snow, and, perhaps, like Mount Senis in Savoy, is hardly ever free from it.

On the 16th, about ten in the morning, we steered west by south, with a fine breeze,

At

at the distance of about three miles from shore. We saw Mowee about two o'clock in the afternoon, about seven leagues distant. The weather was now perfectly clear, and we had an opportunity of observing the land on the coast of Owhyhee. It has a beautiful appearance, seeming to be formed in distinct plantations, and all in the hightest state of cultivation. Trees of everlasting verdure decorate the higher grounds, and limpid streams meander through the soil, increasing its fertility, and adding to the beauty of the enchanting scene.

Karakakooa having, for several reasons, been thought an improper place to anchor in, a resolution was taken to examine another bay towards the south-west. This bay had been surveyed when Captain Cook was here, and we supposed it would afford a good harbour; but the breeze dying away early in the afternoon, several canoes came about us; in consequence of which we hove to, and purchased of the natives, hogs, plantains, potatoes, &c. A most seasonable supply! many of our people being much afflicted with the scurvy. It is indeed surprising, considering how little fresh provision we had lately had, that the complaint was not more general.

During

During the night of the 16th, the weather was extremely sultry, attended with much lightning, and a dead calm; but a breeze sprung up in the morning of the 17th, and we stood for the bay which has been mentioned: but, wishing to purchase as many necessaries as possible, the commodore sent one of his mates to examine the bay, and the ships lay to, in order to traffic with the natives. The mate returned, and gave very substantial reasons why there was no safe anchorage in it. Upon this information, we abandoned every idea of anchoring at Owhyhee, though it was our intention, if the wind would permit, to continue some time about this part of the island, well knowing that hogs in abundance might be procured.

Among other curiosities brought for sale by the natives, were small circular baskets, beautifully wrought, the wicker-work being curiously variegated with scarlet twigs. These are probably of a new manufacture, as nothing of this kind was shewn when Captain Cook visited these regions.

In the afternoon of the 19th, Mowee then bearing west, it was resolved to make the easterly point, and come to an anchor there, but

but contrary winds would not permit us to abide by that refolution.

After playing off and on, and occafionally coming to an anchor near the fhore, in expectation of being attended by canoes with hogs and vegetables, we faw Owhyhee at the diftance of about feven leagues, and came to a refolution to make it as foon as poffible. A frefh breeze fprung up on the evening of the 25th from the fouthward, which continued almoft unabated during the 26th and 27th. Afterwards it continued hanging to the fouthward, and we now gave up all intentions of making Owhyhee.

Not being above a league from Morotoy, on the 28th feveral canoes approached us, bringing a few fmall hogs and fome vegetables: but this fupply was fo inadequate to our wants, that we came to a refolution of fteering for Whahoo. We faw that ifland in the morning of the 29th, and at noon the Eaft Hummock bore weft fouth-weft, about the diftance of eight leagues.

In the forenoon of the 30th, we ftood fouth-weft, with a fine breeze at fouth-eaft. The weft end of Morotoy bore fouth-eaft, and Whahoo fouth-weft, diftant about two leagues.

leagues. At six in the afternoon we anchored in the bay we lay in before, and at no great distance from our old situation. In the evening we moored ship with the stream anchor and cable.

On the 1st of December we received the early visits of a great number of canoes, chiefly laden with water, which they disposed of on the same moderate terms as before. Some hogs and vegetables were also brought us, but not proportionate to our wishes, or even our necessities. Anxious to know the cause, we were informed that those articles had been tabooed till the king had been on board our vessels, and that his arrival was very shortly expected. We had completed our water on the 3d, at two o'clock in the afternoon; and the natives were desirous of bringing more, so delighted were they with the reward they obtained for their labour.

Teereteere. the king, honoured us with a visit on the 4th. He came in a double canoe, attended by two nephews, and many other chiefs. The king has a respectable appearance, is tall, and well-proportioned, but seems to have weak eyes. His age is about forty-eight years. His nephews were incontestibly the finest fellows we had seen in any of the islands. The elder was named Piapia, and the younger Myaro. Piapia is indeed somewhat disfigured by the loss of three of his fore-teeth, but he is otherwise a very graceful personage. It was not, however, in battle that he was deprived of his teeth: he voluntarily parted with them, as a token of respect to the memory of three departed friends; it being the custom here for those who are chiefs, to part with a tooth on the death of a near relation, or any other person whom they tenderly regarded. His arms and legs are curiously tatooed.

Myaro, the other nephew, is erect, delicate, graceful, and majestic; and his countenance is animated and expressive. Teereteere, after receiving some trifling presents from Captain Dixon, quitted the vessel about three o'clock in the afternoon. Soon after his return, we were much more abundantly supplied with hogs and vegetables than we had been before, which we attributed to his influence among the people: and there cannot be a doubt but we attributed it to the real cause.

During the 5th and 6th we were all engaged in business—some were employed in taking in wood from the natives, which they
cheerfully

cheerfully fupplied us with, on the fame moderate terms, that they furnifhed us with water ; others were killing and falting the hogs; and fome were engaged in the very neceffary bufinefs of overhauling the rigging and repairing it.

CHAP.

CHAP. VI.

Visited by Teereteera, king of Whahoo.—The natives attempt to steal the whale-boat.—A priest comes on board—his method of taking the ava.—Account of an human sacrifice.—The injustice of Teereteera.—Piapia resolves to come to England.—Depart from Atoui.

ON the 7th, 8th, 9th, and 10th of December, the wind blew fresh, and the sea ran too high for us to expect to be visited by many of the natives; but the king and his attendants came on board several times during those four days. He never omitted bringing some trivial matter with him, by way of present; but he was trebly overpaid by the generosity of the captain. It was indeed extremely necessary to purchase his friendship and protection, as we knew he could have tabooed the inhabitants at his pleasure, and not suffer a canoe to approach the ships.

Our whale-boat, while we remained at anchor in this harbour, was generally secured to the ship's stern. Strict attention was paid to her, to prevent her being stolen; but in the evening of the 11th, before the rising of the moon, several canoes were observed about her. The captain therefore instantly

stantly fired a musket over them, and they fled with precipitation.

The next day we caught a large shark, and made a present of it to the king, who in return sent a fine hog on board by his son. The youth, however, possessing more craft than honesty or honour, sold us the hog for a large toe; suppressing the circumstance of its having been expressly sent by the father as an equivalent for the shark.

Having observed a bay to the westward of our situation, which seemed to promise a good harbour, the commodore sent three of the officers in his long-boat to survey it. On their return, which was early in the morning on the 15th, they reported that they could find no good anchorage in any part of that bay.

Among the few visitors who were permitted to come on board, an old priest made his appearance, whose authority we found was very considerable. He never came without two attendants, one of which prepared his Ava, and the other waited on him as a servant. Though Captain Cook has mentioned the Ava, and the manner of taking it, a few words upon that subject may not be unnecessary. The Ava is a root used solely

solely by the chiefs, and is thus prepared by a servant kept entirely for that purpose. He chews a sufficient quantity till it is well masticated, then puts it into a wooden bowl, pours a little water over it, and strains the liquor through a cloth. Thus prepared, the Aree or chief drinks it with a degree of eagerness and satisfaction. This beverage creates intoxication, accompanied with a kind of stupefaction, and is probably as pernicious, as an Englishman would think it filthy and disgusting. From the use of that, or some other cause, the priest appeared much emaciated and diseased, his body being covered with a whitish scurf.

In the morning of the 14th we saw a number of natives busily employed on a distant hill; and about noon the next day they were so advanced in their work, that we could perceive they had been building a house. The same afternoon we were deserted by all the canoes, and none of them returned to us in the evening. We were somewhat surprized at this circumstance; because, on every preceding evening, several women came on board, and continued with our men the whole night: this intercourse being allowed, because it could not be prevented.

It

It is certain that the people were tabooed, for, on the 16th, not a single canoe was to be seen in the bay; but round the spot where the temporary edifice was erected, the people were very numerous; and in the evening several large fires were made at a small distance from that structure.

On the 14th, about ten in the morning, a man came on board with a small pig as a present, and also gave us a branch of the cocoa-palm: the priest too paid us a second visit; and about noon Teereteere arrived, bringing with him a hog, and some cocoa-nuts. Plenty of canoes now came about us, and we were convinced that the taboo was taken off; but we could not obtain any certain intelligence why it was laid on. We were informed, however, that some solemn festival had been held on the summit of the hill; and we gathered, from different information, that there had been an offering of a human sacrifice, but of what sex we could not learn. The women still continued under the operation of the taboo, and none of them were permitted to approach the ships.

About two o'clock in the morning of the 10th, a sudden gust of wind parted our small bower cable; but after much difficulty and trouble, we found the anchor, and

and got in on board in the morning of the 19th. We were now pretty well supplied with hogs and vegetables; but no women were permitted to come on board the ships, and we were made acquainted with the reason. A woman had been detected eating pork in one of the vessels, from which they are always tabooed on shore; her crime was considered of the first magnitude, and she really became a sacrifice to appease the wrath of their deities, for so atrocious an offence. This ceremony occasioned so many people to assemble on the mountain, and the strict taboo that had been imposed. There was, however, another reason for their being so numerous. The king had ordered the house to be erected on the hill, to serve as a repository for the various articles which the natives might receive from our ships. When the building was completed, orders were issued from him for every one to bring the things he had procured, to his store-house, and there deposit them. These orders were instantly obeyed, and the conscientious king framed a plausible pretext to keep half of them for his own use. This conduct was so opposite to equity and justice, that the priest did not scruple, when on board the Queen Charlotte, to express his detestation of it in the most pointed terms, and flatly charged him with

with deceit and fraud. It appears, however, from this tranfaction, that the king has abfolute authority.

In the morning of the 20th, we weighed anchor and made fail, and at noon we were about ten miles from the bay. Piapia, the king's nephew, was on board the commodore's fhip, accompanied by Teereteere's Ava-chewer. Piapia was indeed fo much attached to the commodore, that he refolved to go to England with him; and the attendant expreffed an inclination to go with him. Several canoes, in which were many of the relations of the two adventurers, followed the King George to a confiderable diftance from Whahoo; and, at their feparation, which they fuppofed for ever, they teftified their grief by their lamentations, wringing of hands, and other expreffive tokens and gefticulations. Piapia and his fervant fhewed fome concern at parting; but their attention was almoft wholly occupied on their new adventure.

At noon on the 22d, the ifland Oneehow bore weft fouth-weft; Wymoa Bay, where we propofed to anchor, being to the fouthward. About four o'clock in the afternoon, Captain Portlock came to anchor, and we prepared to do the fame at a convenient diftance. We found no bottom with eighty fathom line, and being unavoidably drifted to leeward, we could not make the situation we at first proposed; but at six o'clock we came to a good situation in eighteen fathom water, almost a league from the King George, and above a mile from shore.

When these islands were discovered by Captain Cook, he first anchored at Atoui, where he found hogs and vegetables in great abundance. In the morning of the 23d of December, canoes came round us in great numbers, laden with hogs, cocoa-nuts, and vegetables. They were very moderate in their expectations for roots and nuts; but, finding us pretty eager in purchasing large hogs, their demands were at first exorbitant for such as came under that description; but, upon our appearing indifferent, they grew more reasonable in their prices, and we could buy one of their largest hogs for one or two toes. On our requesting them to procure us water, they brought us some of a most excellent quality, and continued to supply us on the same moderate terms that the inhabitants of Whahoo had done. The regular price of cocoa-nuts was five for a smallish nail. The taro and the sugar-cane were plentiful, fine, and cheap.

On

On the 25th, being Christmas-day, we had much conviviality and good cheer; and, as usual, toasted our friends and mistresses.

The weather was variable, but moderate, till the 4th of January 1787, by which time we had packed five puncheons of salted pork; but hogs were not so plenty as we had found them. We suspected this scarcity to be artificial. From the 4th to the 9th, we were barely supplied with a sufficiency for our immediate consumption.

Besides the articles for food, the natives traded largely in fishing lines, mats, cloaks, necklaces, caps, and many other curiosities. Numbers of beautiful bird-skins, finely preserved, were also offered to us. At our request, they furnished us with many of these birds alive: they have a long beak, the wings and back are brown, and the breast and throat of a shining red; their size does not exceed that of a sparrow. They are certainly a species of the humming-bird, described by Pennant. We paid so liberally for these, that a variety of other birds were brought, and, among them, a species of the teal, or wild duck.

Concluding from hence, that plenty of
game

game might be found upon the ifland, and being fond of the diverfion of fhooting, Captain Dixon took his gun on fhore, attended by only one fervant in an Indian canoe. He was apprehenfive, however, that he fhould not experience much fport, fuppofing the curiofity of the natives would induce them to crowd about him: but he found himfelf miftaken, for the inhabitants applied themfelves fo clofely to their manufactures and other employments, that they could not find leifure to obferve his proceedings; he therefore traverfed the country at his eafe, and met with no kind of interruption. But game were not fo plentiful as he expected, though he generally returned with a few of the trophies of the field.

Our wood was, by this time, confiderably reduced; we therefore applied to the natives to procure us fome: they readily engaged to furnifh us with any quantity, nearly on the terms we were fupplied with that article at Whahoo, though the natives here were obliged to fetch it from the mountains. So great a value did they fet on iron, that they brought even their poles, rafters, and fences for fale: fome of them even demolifhed part of their habitations, and exchanged for a fmall quantity of that eftimable metal.

In

In the morning of the 10th of January, the commodore made the fignal for weighing anchor; but we were at that time becalmed, and could not poffibly anfwer his fignal; Captain Portlock therefore came again to anchor where he had before been ftationed.

A ftrong breeze fpringing up, we weighed at fix o'clock in the morning, on the 11th, and made fail for Oneehow, where we expected to have come to anchor by four o'clock; but the wind proving unfavourable, we could not even attempt it. After many difficulties and difappointments, we again made for Oneehow, the wind happening to fuit, and anchored in Yam-Bay, in the afternoon of the 26th.

The wind blew fo frefh on the 27th, at north north-eaft, that our fituation was far from being agreeable. We were principally induced to come to Oneehow, to lay in a ftock of yams, they being the only root in that ifland which will keep for any length of time. The furf ran fo very high as to deter the canoes from coming near us. The King George laying about two miles from us, we hove up our anchor on the 28th, and came to at a convenient diftance from her;

her; soon after which we were informed, that the commodore, during the last gale, was obliged to cut his cables and run to sea, and found it extremely difficult to weather the breakers at the north point of the Bay.

CHAP. VII.

Proceed to Wymoa-Bay, Atoui—Are visited by Abbenoue and his son—The king comes on board—Several officers of the ship take a little tour up the country—Several of the officers entertained by Abbenoue.

AT two o'clock on the 29th, the wind being westerly, Captain Portlock made a signal for weighing anchor, and by three we made sail. The wind shifting to north-west, we determined to make Wymoa-Bay, Atoui: this we accomplished, and anchored there about ten o'clock. We moored here with both bowers on the 31st, intending to stay while the weather would permit; this bay being much more eligible than the road at Oneehow.

Abbenoue, whom we had before seen at Oneehow, came often on board, and rendered us many services. When we saw him before, he had a disorder in his eyes, and his body was covered with a whitish scurf; but having, pursuant to our advice, discontinued the use of that filthy beverage ava, he appeared healthy, vigorous, and active. He had a son named Tyheira, who also seemed inclined to assist us, but we found he acted from mercenary motives, and was in every respect less estimable than his father. We

I   were

were much indebted to two other chiefs for their goods offices, their influence having procured us great quantities of hogs and vegetables.

For several days we received all our supplies from these chiefs, none of inferior rank coming near us. They informed us that the common people had been tabooed, and could not furnish us with water, or any other article, till the king had been on board our ships. We could not learn the cause of this taboo being imposed, but conjectured it was meant in order to exact a kind of tribute from the common people, for permitting them to traffic with us.

The king paid us a visit on the 5th of February, in a large double canoe, with a numerous retinue. Piapia, who went from Whahoo with the commodore, was one of the attendants: he had abandoned the idea of going to England, and was resolved to remain at Atoui. When we anchored there, and went ashore, he found himself among his friends and relations, many of whom he had never before seen. It is not therefore to be wondered at that he changed his resolution.

The king, who now honoured us with his

his prefence, is named Tiara. He much refembles Teereteere, king of Whahoo, who is his brother, but furpaffes him greatly in knowledge and underftanding. He afked feveral fhrewd and pertinent queftions refpecting the management of the fhip; and particularly requefted to know which point of the compafs pointed towards England, and the diftance we then were from it. Before he quitted the veffel, Captain Dixon made him a prefent of fome beads and toes, with which he feemed well pleafed, and affured us that his people fhould be permitted to trade with us, as before that injunction had taken place. We were foon convinced of his having performed his promife, by the attendance of the canoes, laden with hogs, water, vegetables, and curiofities.

On the 9th of February, I accompanied feveral of our people on fhore, by way of amufement and recreation. Not being able to land from our boat, on account of a great furf, canoes were politely provided for us, and we were landed fafely, commodioufly, and expeditioufly. Before we proceeded on our little tour, Abbenoue conducted us to a place, to let us fee what was preparing for our dinner. His fervants were employed in cleaning a fine hog, which he informed us was to be baked, and he pointed to some taro, which was meant to be eaten with it. He wished to be informed if there was enough for us, and, being answered in the affirmative, he expressed much satisfaction.

He then entreated us not to go too far, as the hour for dining was twelve o'clock, which he significantly explained by pointing to the sun.

Having heard frequent mention of a village which the natives called A Tappo, where a manufacture of cloth was carried on, some of us proposed to make that the place of our destination, as the distance was not more than three miles.

The inhabitants, prompted by curiosity, crouded about us on our first landing, but our people walking different ways, the natives divided into parties, and none of us were much incommoded. One man tendered his services to shew us the way to A Tappo, and to attend us the whole day for a large nail. We agreed, and he conducted us thither. It is a large village, judiciously situated behind a long row of cocoa-nut trees, which sheltered the inhabitants from the immoderate heat of the sun in its meridian.

We

We were disappointed in our expectations of seeing the inhabitants at work in their respective manufactures. When we arrived there, they quitted their labour and gathered eagerly about us, intreating us to accept of the little kindnesses they were enabled to bestow: some ran to the trees to gather cocoa-nuts, which they presented to us with great complacency and respect; others intreated us to repose ourselves under the shady branches of the trees, which were planted before their little mansions; some kindly furnished us with water to allay our thirst. Every one was active in relieving our wants, or endeavouring to contribute to our satisfaction.

Thinking we should be too late for dinner if we continued any longer at A Tappa, we agreed to return; and, at that instant saw Tyheira, who had two reasons for following us to this village; one, to hinder the people from incommoding us, and the other, to acquaint us that the repast would be ready by the time we got back to our landing place. He afterwards meanly requested us to make him a present for his care and attention, and collected five or six nails. The power which these chiefs have over the common people is astonishing: Tyheira threw stones at some of the natives, large
enough

enough to have lamed or maimed them; but they bore it with the moſt patient ſubmiſſion and humility.

Dinner was almoſt ready on our return to the appointed ſpot, and a large houſe was put in order for our reception. Four perſons were employed in ſerving up our rapaſt. One was loaded with a calabaſh of water; another brought in a parcel of cocoa-nuts; a third ſtalked along with a bowl full of baked taro; and the laſt, preceded by Tyheira himſelf, cloſed the proceſſion, with a hog, on a large circular wooden diſh. The bearer of the hog, in order to make gravy, poured water over it, and rubbed it with his hands. We did not much approve of that method of making ſauce; but we all made a moſt excellent dinner, and the cook had done his part to perfection.

Attendants were provided to open cocoa-nuts for us, when we were thirſty, and every thing was conducted with decency, decorum, and even elegance. After dinner ſeveral of our gentlemen amuſed themſelves with walking, and in the evening went on board; Abbenoue's people being ready to paddle us through the ſurf to our boat, which was then at anchor waiting for us.

In

In the afternoon and evening of the 10th of February, the weather was very squally, accompanied with thunder, lightning, and heavy rain, the wind at south-west. Finding the weather very unpromising, it was thought necessary to quit this place, and early in the morning of the 12th, the commodore making a signal, we weighed anchor, and stretched to the southward. On the 16th we stood right for Oneehow, and in the afternoon anchored in Yam-Bay, distant about two miles from shore.

CHAP. VIII.

Arrive at Wymoa Bay, Atoui—find the inhabitants tabooed.—Attempt to make Owhyhee—Steer for the American coast.—Arrive at Prince William's Sound.—Captain Dixon takes an excursion in a whale-boat.—Find the Nootka, Capt. Meares, in a creek.

WE had not been long here before we were attended by a great number of canoes, which brought us large quantities of yams; an article we much wanted, having nearly expended all our roots. In the afternoon of the 17th, the wind being to the southward, we weighed anchor, intending to make Atoui, should the southerly winds continue.

Early in the morning of the 26th, we worked through the passage between Oruhoura and Atoui. On the 27th we had fresh breezes and variable weather; and early on the 28th, having a moderate breeze from the east, we came to anchor in Wymoa Bay. The weather being fine on the 1st of March, we expected the natives to come about us with a supply of hogs and vegetables; but we were only attended by a few of the inferior chiefs, who informed us that the inhabitants were tabooed. The chiefs

chiefs however brought us a small quantity of taro.

We were apprehensive, and perhaps not without reason, that the king wanted to get rid of us, and had therefore tabooed the people, to prevent our receiving any refreshments: he perhaps suspected, from our frequent visits, that we intended to take up our abode in Atoui; and, like a prudent general, was determined to starve us out. In the evening we weighed anchor, and stood out to sea.

The weather proved foggy on the 3d, 4th, and 5th, which induced us to lay to. The armourer set to work to prepare some articles of traffic, but unfortunately his anvil fell overboard by a sudden roll of the ship: we lamented this accident, having but few toes remaining.

Having fresh easterly breezes on the 6th and 7th, we steered east south-east, meaning to make Owhyhee, if the wind continued in the same quarter; but, on its veering to the east, we abandoned that intention.

On the 11th in the afternoon, having a steady easterly breeze, and being within

two

two miles of Whahoo, on the weſtern ſide, we lay to, in expectation of being furniſhed with proviſion; but only two anoes caime near us, and they had hardly any thng to diſpoſe of.

We ſtood to the weſtward, and early in the morning of the 12th, ſaw Atoui: about noon we were in Wymoa Bay, not far from where we had before anchored, and ſtood on under an eaſy ſail, hoping the inhabitants would bring us ſome hogs and vegetables; but not a canoe appeared. This was an additional proof that Tiara was determined to ſtarve us from his dominions. We therefore deſpaired of procuring any quantity of hogs, but hoped to obtain a ſupply of yams from Oneehow:— that however depended on the wind.

Towards the evening of the 13th, the ſky grew black and lowering, and the air was alſo intolerably ſultry. It rained inceſſantly during the whole night, and the ſtorm was accompanied with thunder and lightning to a tremendous degree. On the 14th we had alternately light airs and calms; but in the afternoon, a freſh breeze ſprung up at north eaſt, on which we hauled our wind to the ſouthward, expecting early in the morning to bear away for Oneehow;

Oneehow; but, in the morning, the wind shifted to south-east; when Captain Portlock hauled his wind, and steered north-east. In the morning of the 16th we had cleared all the islands, and steered due north for the American coast.

In the morning of the 17th, we had a brisk southerly breeze; in the afternoon the wind was variable, and in the night we had several squalls, with thunder, lightning, and incessant rain.

We had a heavy gale of wind in the morning of the 18th, with rain, and a prodigious swell. The gale continued the whole day, and a considerable part of the night, when it was so very dark that we lay to. We made sail at five the next morning, the weather being then pretty moderate.

From the 19th to the 23d the wind was fresh and variable; on the 24th and 25th we had frequent squalls. We had then clear moderate weather till the evening of the 29th, when a fresh gale sprung up from the west. The weather grew moderate in the morning of the 31st, and in the afternoon we had light variable airs. In the evening we saw several puffins, a young seal

seal appeared along-side; certain indications that land could not be far off; but the weather was so foggy, that it must have been at no great distance when we could discern it.

On the 1st, 2d, 3d, and 4th of April, it blew fresh, with very little variety, from south-east to south-west. The nights being very dark, we generally lay to, and made sail early in the morning. On the 7th, we saw a great many birds, among which were gulls and divers; and, on the 8th, a sea-lion was observed playing about the vessel.

From the 9th to the 16th, we had fresh variable winds with sleet and snow. The weather was immoderately cold; on the 16th, the thermometer was two degrees and a half lower than it had ever been in Captain Cook's last voyage. From the 16th to the 18th, the weather was so hazy that we could not get an observation; nor could we discern land at any distance; we therefore plied occasionally, not knowing how far we were from the American coast.

On the 18th, towards the evening, we had a sudden squall, but received no injury. The wind blew a fresh gale during the night;

night; but it moderated the next morning, and the weather was so clear as to permit us to take a meridian altitude. On the 20th, 21st, and 22d, it was hazy, and we had plenty of snow and sleet. We plied with the greatest caution, well knowing that the coast could not be far off, and we could not see land were it within the distance of a league.

Early in the morning of the 23d, the weather was pretty clear, and at noon we perceived land at about ten leagues distance, bearing from north-east to west. At noon we saw land from north-east to west, about ten leagues distant. In the evening we were convinced that the land to the west was Foot Island, and that to the east Mountague Island; consequently we were standing well for Prince William's Sound, which we attempted to make when we were last upon this coast. Towards the close of the evening, the south-east part of Mountague Island stood north 32 deg. east, about five leagues distant. In the morning of the 24th, having a moderate breeze from the west, we set sail, and stood in right for the passage, and at noon we were right in the entrance of the channel. This place is erroneously laid down in Captain Cook's
general

general charts, which was now ascertained by a careful observation.

In the afternoon we had a calm, and consequently were unable to reach the Sound; we therefore stood into a deep bay, which now opened to the east, and came to anchor at six in the evening.

Our commodore was partly induced to come to anchor, from his seeing two canoes at a pretty considerable distance up the bay. He was convinced that we were not far from inhabitants, and thought it probable we might have some traffick with them.

Five canoes attended us in the afternoon of the 24th, but without furs or any other commercial article. The people saluted us with friendly gesticulations, and we returned the salutation. On our asking for *Notooneshuc*, a term they use for otters' skin, they frequently and earnestly repeated the words *Nootka Notooneshuc*, at the same time pointing towards Prince William's Sound. Some dogs on board, hearing the voices of strangers, began to bark at them. The Indians immediately called out, *Towzer, Towzer, here!*—and whistled like the English

lish, when they endeavour to entice a dog to come near them.

From hearing these people speak English, we conjectured that some British vessel lay in the Sound at that time, or had lately been in that situation.

The ears of these people were decorated with a number of blue beads, which we supposed they had been furnished with by the Russians: we were confirmed in this opinion, when they displayed some iron weapons, which bore evident marks of Russian fabrication.

In the morning of the 25th our boats were sent on shore for wood and water, which were both procured without difficulty. Our captains in the mean time went round the bay, but found no inhabitants nor habitations; whence we concluded, that our visitors were only wanderers from Prince William's Sound. We presented them with some trifles, as an inducement for them to bring us some furs, and to prevail on others to do the same. They seemed to have a grateful sense of the favours which had been conferred on them, and promised to return speedily, and bring with them a large quantity of skins.

We

We waited, in anxious expectation of a second visit from these Indians, till the 28th; but we beheld them no more. In the morning of the 29th, having a fine breeze at south-west, we unmoored and stood out of the bay, but when we had reached the channel leading into the Sound, we were becalmed. The tide was against us, and we were obliged to tow the vessels in again. At eleven we came to anchor in twenty fathom water. On the 30th the weather was moderate, but we received no visits from the Indians. Geese, ducks, gulls, and variety of smaller birds, were plenty in this bay, but they were too shy to suffer us to come within musket shot of them. A species of polypus, possessing both an animal and vegetable substance, was taken here by our people, with a hook and line.

On the 1st of May, having a breeze at south-west, we unmoored at two o'clock, and stood up the channel towards Prince William's Sound. At six, being close in shore, and a calm coming on, we anchored in a bay to the eastward. In the morning of the 2d, having a breeze at southwest, we weighed anchor and stood for the channel, between Montague and Green Islands; a dangerous passage, in night or bad

bad weather, being in no part a mile in breadth free from sunken rocks. In the evening, a light breeze enabled us to get into a bay in Montague Island, and came to about nine o'clock.

Being now in a secure harbour, it was agreed on that the two ships should be severally hawled on shore, that their bottoms might be thoroughly scrubbed and cleaned. During this operation, Capt. Dixon took the Queen Charlotte's whale-boat, and the King George's whale-boat and long-boat, to go in search of trade, wherever he thought it probable he might find inhabitants. Care was taken however to have all the boats well manned and armed, and his excursion was attended with some remarkable circumstances; the substance of which we shall relate, as it was communicated to us on the captain's return:

His primary intention was to make Hinchinbroke Cove, but bad weather rendered it necessary to put into a cove in Montague Island, about eight o'clock in the evening; but, as the weather grew moderate about nine, he proceeded to a large bay, near the north-east end of the island. Here he saw some Indians, who told him they belonged to Cape Hinchinbrooke,

brooke, but were then on a hunting party. Growing late, the captain came to an anchor in the long boat, to which the whale-boats were made faſt, one on each ſide. The Indians continued to ſkulk near this ſpot, after night came on; therefore ſix hands were ordered to keep watch, and the reſt to have their arms ready in caſe of a ſurprize.

Captain Dixon weighed early in the morning, and anchored at Cape Hinchinbrooke about eleven, where he ſaw ſeveral Indians, and bought ſome otter-ſkins. Theſe were of a different tribe from thoſe he met with in the bay north-eaſt of Montague Iſland; their behaviour was daring and inſolent, and they ſeemed inclined to attack the captain and his little crew. They did not, however, quit the boats till day-light the next morning, and then paddled away, ſeemingly diſconcerted and diſſatisfied. The captain and his guard found it neceſſary to be extremely vigilant during the whole night.

Early in the morning, he ſet off for Snug-Corner cove; but there was ſo little wind, that the whale-boat, were obliged to tow the long-boat and he did not arrive at the place of deſtination till ten o'clock o'clock at night. He saw no inhabitants, at that time; but he ordered a strict watch to be kept, recollecting that the Discovery was boarded by the Indians in this very cove, even in open day, during Captain Cook's last voyage.

He saw none of the natives, till daylight on the 8th, when two of them appeared in a canoe, acquainting him that there was a ship at some little distance, and tendering their services to conduct him to it for a present of some beads. He readily embraced their offer, and set off with the whale-boats; leaving the long-boat at anchor, fearing it might retard his progress. The weather soon grew very bad, and his guides deserted him. He continued the search, however, till almost noon; but heavy squalls, and storms of snow and sleet, made him resolve to return to the long-boat, where he arrived about four in the afternoon.

Six canoes came into the cove about seven o'clock. The captain was again informed that there was a vessel not far off, and the Indians offered to be his guides; he went with them in his own long-boat, leaving the other two in the cove. At ten he saw the vessel in a creek. She was a snow,

snow, called the Nootka, from Bengal, commanded by Captain Meares: She had sailed from Bengal in March 1786, and touched at Oonalaſka in Auguſt. Captain Meares then informed Captain Dixon, that he found a paſſage to Cook's River through Whitſuntide Bay, and that he ſaw ſome Ruſſian ſettlers, who told him they had a ſettlement at a place called Codiac; that two European veſſels then lay at Codiac, and that two other ſhips had been lately ſeen in Cook's River.

After receiving this intelligence, he reſolved to ſteer for Prince William's Sound, and arrived there late in the month of September.

Captain Meares had wintered in the creek where he then was; and the ſcurvy had made terrible devaſtation among his people: two of his mates, the ſurgeon, and a great number of the foremaſt men, had been carried off by that malignant diſorder, and the reſt were rendered ſo feeble by its attacks, that Captain Meares was the only man on board able to walk the decks.

He expreſſed great ſatisfaction on being informed two veſſels were ſo near him, who would

would doubtlefs afford him fuccour or relief. Captain Dixon affured him he might depend upon being furnifhed with fuch neceffaries as he and Captain Portlock could fpare.

Captain Dixon quitted the Nootka early in the morning of the 9th, and got to his boats at nine: at eleven he ftood for the fhips, and, as he croffed the Sound, fome canoes came round him; and one of the Indians had a few fea otter-fkins to difpofe of. Obferving a frying-pan in the longboat, he defired to have that in exchange for his fkins: his terms were complied with, and the frying-pan tendered to him. He defired fome of the captain's people to break off the handle, which he took, and with which he feemed exceedingly delighted, and threw the bottom part away. Very rough and ftormy weather came on afterwards, with inceffant fnow and fleet; and Captain Dixon did not arrive on board the Queen Charlotte till four o'clock in the morning, on the 10th of May.

In the morning of the 10th, Captain Meares, and his firft mate, went in their own boat on board the King George, having feveral bags of rice with them, to exchange for fuch articles as might moft be wanted.

wanted. They informed us that the fur trade had been carried on for some years, from different parts of the East-Indies. They related many extraordinary stories respecting their great success; but, as the captain and mate varied materially in their accounts, we gave but little credit to their tales. They, doubtless, might have procured a vast quantity of good furs, and those, perhaps, chiefly in Prince William's Sound.

Captain Meares and his mate left the captains Portlock and Dixon about noon on the 10th, having first received a seasonable supply of brandy, molasses, sugar, flour, and some other articles which we could spare. The commodore even spared Captain Meares a couple of his seamen, to assist in conducting his vessel to the Sandwich Islands.

We now had a sufficient clue to enable us to judge of the meaning of those Indians who repeated the word Nootka, and pointed towards Prince William's Sound. Nor was it any longer a matter of surprize that they had spoken English; for one of them, as we were informed, had been on board the Nootka several weeks.

On the 11th, all hands were employed in

in ſtowing the hold, and getting in wood and water. The armourers of both veſſels had a tent on ſhore, and were buſily employed in fabricating toes, though they had but one anvil between them; but they applied themſelves to the different ſtages of the article they were manufacturing; one forged and faſhioned it, the other filed and poliſhed it.

CHAP IX.

Plan of feparation agreed on—A chief and his people bring a letter—they commit feveral thefts on board—Narrow efcape of a fifhing party—Difcover an excellent harbour, which we named Port Mulgrave—Manners and cuftoms of the inhabitants—Method of difpofing of their dead.

THE better to promote our fuccefs in the laft feafon, which was now approaching, we feparated. Meffieurs Hayward and Hill were difpatched in the commodore's long-boat, to trade in Cook's River. The King George was to remain in Prince William's Sound till that boat returned; and the Queen Charlotte was to fteer for King George's Sound, keeping as near the coaft as poffible, in order to have the better chance of collecting fkins.

In confequence of this arrangement, Meffieurs Hayward and Hill fet out in the afternoon of the 12th of May, with a proper affortment of trading articles. Soon after their departure, two canoes came up to us, in both of which there were eleven people. Though they brought us nothing, they promifed to come heavy laden the next day, and that their chief fhould be of the party.

Thinking

Thinking it probable that the Indians might return, and the wind being variable, several of our people were sent in the whale-boat in purfuit of fifh; and others were permitted to amufe themfelves on fhore. About noon feveral canoes were perceived at a confiderable diftance, in which were a great many of the Indians. When they approached the veffel, they began to fing, the ftrokes of their paddles correfponding in exact time with their voices. The chief appeared to be the leader of this vocal band, and the concert was not inharmonious. After much ceremony, when they came along fide the King George, the chief produced a letter for Captain Portlock, brought from on board the Nootka. The chief, whofe name was Stanway, was therefore admitted on board, with feveral of his people.

The letter had been written by Captain Meares before we had feen him, in confequence of being informed, by fome of thefe people, that they had feen two veffels at anchor down the channel. He difpatched them immediately with this letter, without any addrefs, they promifing to return with an anfwer, with the greateft expedition. They had, however, neglected this bufinefs till the epiftle became ufelefs.

The

The commodore admitted Stanway's people on board from prudential motives, imagining he should secure their favour by such indulgence, and induce them to trade largely with him; but it soon appeared that they had other objects in view more than that of traffic; those few articles they had were damaged, and of no value. They considered the letter as an introduction on board, which would enable them to exercise their talent of pilfering. They managed the business, however, with much art and dexterity. Stanway, and some of his people, amused the King George's people with singing and dancing, whilst others were busied in traversing the decks, and stealing every thing within their reach, which they threw to their companions who remained in the canoes. Unwilling to take severe measures upon this occasion, Captain Portlock stationed his people in different parts of the vessel to watch them, and put a stop to their depredations. Still they ventured to exercise themselves in their favourite business; and even when they were detected, they exhibited no tokens of concern or sense of shame, thinking they had acquitted themselves with honour by returning the things they had stolen. Iron and cloaths were the first objects of their plunder; but, finding they were watched,
they

they took every thing they could find, and did not quit the place till about six o'clock in the afternoon.

Our whale-boat, in which the people were fishing, lay at anchor about two miles distant: this the Indians observed, and made directly towards them. Alarmed at this circumstance, the commodore manned his whale-boat and yawl, and went to the assistance of the fishing party, supposing their lives would be in danger; the Indians being well armed with knives and spears. The yawl was also dispatched from the Queen Charlotte; and Captain Dixon, at that instant, fired a swivel, at which the Indians seems terrified, and immediately paddled off.

Our fears were not merely imaginary, for when the people returned from fishing, we were informed, that the Indians had endeavoured to steal their anchor, and actually stole some of their fishing lines. One of them even attempted to stab a young fellow with his spear, for refusing to part with his line, but was with-held by Stanway. The anglers, however, caught a pretty large quantity of sand dabs, and some rock fish.

About noon on the 14th, the wind being

ing south-west, we stood up the channel for Prince William's Sound; and by two in the afternoon we saw the north point of Montague Island. About four, Captain Dixon went on board the King George, to take leave of the commodore, being near the spot where we had agreed to separate. About eight he returned to his ship, and we parted company with colours flying, and three hearty cheers.

Early in the morning of the 15th, Cape Hinchinbrooke bore north-west, about seven leagues distant; whales in great abundance were seen about the ship; at eight in the evening we saw Kay's Island. On the 17th and 18th, we had moderate variable winds; and in the afternoon of the latter we beheld Mount Elias. In the evening of the 19th we had a strong breeze and heavy swell.

On the 20th, 21st, and 22d, we had moderate variable weather. At three in the morning of the 23d, we stood in for the westernmost point of land, and at five we were within two miles of shore. About half after six, one of our mates was sent into a bay in the north-east, in search of anchoring ground. He returned between eight and nine, with the pleasing intelligence

gence that he had found a good harbour, and seen a multitude of inhabitants. The wind sinking, we found it impracticable to get to the desired station by day-light, and came to at eight o'clock in sixty fathom water. While we were warping into the bay, several canoes came round us, and the people in them seemed to be of a different nation from those we had seen in Prince William's Sound; their canoes were also very differently constructed. Southward of our situation, we saw a narrow creek, and on the 24th we saw a great many Indians on the beach near the entrance of it, who beckoned us to come on shore. Captain Dixon went to survey the place, and saw a great number of inhabitants, and some temporary huts. Soon after we weighed, and began to ply into the harbour which the mate had found for us, and at two o'clock in the afternoon came to anchor at a small distance from the shore.

Not far from us were two large Indian huts: we were soon attended by some of the inhabitants, among whom was an old man, who brought us several sea otter-skins. This was a pleasing circumstance, and induced us to suppose that no trading party had been in this quarter; but we were soon convinced of the contrary, when they

they exhibited the same kinds of spears, beads, and knives, which we had seen in Prince William's Sound. We were now too sensible that we were only the gleaners of the harvest.

Tho' we continued ten days in the harbour, we could only procure seventeen sea otter-skins, two cloaks of earless marmots, and other inferior skins and slips; altogether hardly sufficient to fill one puncheon. The natives had indeed exhausted their stock of furs. They were also so deliberate and dilatory in their mode of traffic, that much time was taken up in dealing with them for the most trifling articles, such as dirty remnants of sea otter-skins, &c. Their method of dealing was, to raise our expectations, by hinting that they had brought something valuable, and after endeavouring a long time to make advantageous terms for themselves, they produced their commodity: much time was then lost in the completion of the bargain, and a day was frequently spent in the purchase of insignificant articles.

Suppoſing ourselves the first discoverers of this harbour, Captain Dixon named it Port Mulgrave, in honour of Lord Mulgrave. Our anchoring-place is situated in
59 deg.

59 deg. 22 min. North lat. and 140 deg. West long. Here were geese and wild ducks, and Captain Dixon went frequently on shore to amuse himself with shooting.

The number of inhabitants about us did not, perhaps, exceed seventy or eighty: they are in general well shaped, and of the middle size. Like the other inhabitants we have seen upon the coast, they delight in painting their faces with a variety of colours, so that their real complexions are absolutely masked.

By presents and persuasion, we prevailed on a young woman to wash her face and hands, and we were astonished at the effect which that simple operation produced: ruddy health bloomed in her cheeks, and her face and neck were fair. Her eyes were black, piercing, and expressive; each under the canopy of a black semicircular brow, as regular as if it had been pencilled by the hand of a Gainsborough or a Reynolds. The symmetry of the whole face, and the form of the contour, were highly pleasing. To speak without raptures, she came the nearest to a divinity of any female we had seen since our departure from England; and even there she would be ranked among the beautiful.

Some

Some of the women, as a mark of diſtinction, have an apertute in the thick part of the under lip, in which they always wear a piece of wood. The lower part of the face is greatly diſtorted by this ſtrange kind of ornament.

Conception cannot frame any thing more wretched than their huts: poles irregularly fixed into the ground, incloſed with looſe boards, conſtitute their habitations. The holes and chinks, which are pretty numerous, anſwer the purpoſe of a chimney to let out the ſmoke, no aperture being expreſsly made for that purpoſe. The inſide of theſe hovels is filthy and abominable beyond deſcription, and yet the inhabitants are perfectly ſatisfied with their condition, and even enjoy life under theſe ſeeming diſadvantages and inconveniences. They would perhaps erect more comfortable houſes to reſide in, had they a permanent ſituation; but theſe are only temporary reſidences; for when their means of ſupport become ſcarce, the little manſion is taken down, and conveyed in a canoe to ſome more plentiful ſpot, where every man erects his own portable habitation; though a total ſtranger to the name of Palladio or Inigo Jones, and indeed to the orders of architecture.

We

We were furnished with plenty of halibut by the Indians, two of whom were angling for those fish, at the same time and place where many of our people were engaged in the same employment; but, tho' our tackle was infinitely superior to theirs, we were not half so succefsful.

They have a singular method of drefsing their victuals, by laying pieces of flesh, fish, &c. into a kind of wicker basket, over which they put heated stones, and cover it up close.

The disposal of the dead in this country is somewhat extraordinary. After separating the head from the body, they are severally wrapped in furs: the head is put into a kind of square box, and the body into another, which has sufficient length, breadth, and height, to receive it. At each end of the latter, a long thick pole is driven into the earth in a slanting position, so that the upper ends meet, and are fastened with a kind of rope. The box with the head in it, is placed about two feet higher than that which contains the body, on a piece of wood which goes acrofs, and is fixed firmly to each pole. These tombs, if they deserve that name, are decorated according to the fancy of the surviving relations:

lations: some with teeth, and others with the shells of various fishes, but all the poles are painted white. We had no opportunity of seeing the funeral rites performed here, none of the inhabitants happening to die while we were resident on the spot; this account being given from taking a view of their cemetary or general repository for their dead.

CHAP.

CHAP. X.

Quit Port Mulgrave—Anchor in Norfolk Sound—Various proceedings there—Persons, manners, and customs of the inhabitants of Norfolk Sound.

CAPTAIN Dixon, thinking the fur-market exhausted in Port Mulgrave, came to a resolution of quitting it as soon as possible: a breeze sprung up from south-east, in the morning of the 4th of June, and we warped out of the harbour; and at eight we made sail. During the remainder of the 4th, and the whole of the 5th, the winds were moderate and variable.

At five in the afternoon of the 6th, we saw mount St. Elias, which bore north-west, about twenty leagues distant. We had moderate and variable weather from the 7th to the 10th; but on the evening of the latter, and the whole of the 11th, we had a fresh breeze from the west. About three in the afternoon it was hazy, but we saw land at the distance of about four miles.

At two in the morning of the 12th, we stood in for a bay we had seen the preceding day, not far from Cape Edgecombe, which appeared to be an excellent harbour. At five we sent our whale-boat a-head to found. At seven we beheld a large boat full of people, but could not particularly distinguish the objects which were on board: as they drew nearer, we knew it to be an Indian canoe, and, when they came alongside, we found they were inhabitants of the sound we were steering for. About six, we lost the breeze, and the whale-boat was just returned; the yawl was hoisted out, and both boats were employed in towing the vessel into the bay. In the mean time we purchased a few furs of the Indians in the canoe, who informed us that we should meet with plenty of people and furs in the adjacent harbour. We were pleased with this intelligence, though we did not absolutely rely upon the truth of it.

At ten o'clock we saw a bay to the northward, and stood right in for it. One of the mates was sent up the sound in search of a harbour; and another into the bay a-head, to examine the soundings. The person who had been sent to examine the soundings returned about twelve o'clock, informing us that the bay was a commodious place for the vessel to lay in. After making a few short boards, we anchored at twelve o'clock in nine fathom water.

In the afternoon, the other mate returned from

from his survey, acquainting us that he had found several good harbours in many respects, but that the bottom was rocky; the captain therefore determined to keep his present situation: he further informed us, that he had found in a cave a human head in a box, decorated with shells.

Early in the morning of the 13th, several canoes came about us, when the Indians who were on board them spent some time in singing, and afterwards produced a number of fine otter skins, which we purchased of them, and congratulated ourselves upon the prospect of our having an excellent trade. We had a constant succession of traffic till the 16th, when it began to decline, though the Indians then promised to procure a supply of skins from their neighbours.

On the 16th, a fresh gale from the south caused a heavy sea to enter into the bay; but about eleven o'clock at night, the weather grew moderate. From the 17th, to the 21st, we had but little commerce with the inhabitants. An intelligent old man among them informed us, that two ships had anchored there, and shewed us a shirt which some of the people on board had given him, which we found, upon examination, to be made after the Spanish fashion.

Though

Though trade was our principal concern, other neceſſary matters were attended to; parties were occaſionally ſent on ſhore to procure wood and water.

Though the natives were, at firſt, tolerably civil, they afterwards grew troubleſome, and attempted to pick the pockets of our people, and even ſtole their ſaws and axes in the moſt daring manner; nothing indeed but coercive meaſures could reſtrain them from theſe proceedings. This place was diſtinguiſhed by the name of Norfolk Sound, in honour of the duke of Norfolk.

During the greater part of the time we lay here, the weather was moderate. Wild currants, gooſeberries, and raſpberries, were found in great plenty.

The number of inhabitants found here is ſuppoſed to be about five hundred.

The people, in form and features, reſemble thoſe of Port Mulgrave; and the faces of the women are ornamented with paint and wood in the ſame manner. The manners and diſpoſition of the inhabitants, however, ſeem rather to accord with thoſe of the natives about Cook's River, and Prince William's Sound.

We

We could not avoid obferving that they always quitted us about twelve o'clock, and went on fhore, where they were engaged about an hour in eating; an evident proof that they have a certain time of dining, which is regulated by the fun. They alfo left us about half an hour after four in the afternoon; but not with that precifion and regularity.

Their apparel is compofed of fkins fewed together in various forms and fafhions. One of their chiefs obtained a prefent from fome of our people, of a Sandwich Ifland cloth, and the next day appeared along-fide of our fhip, dreffed in a coat which had been made of it, cut in a form not unlike that of a waggoner's frock in England, and feemed as proud of his habit, as a London common-council man, when he firft appears in his mazarine gown.

Exclufive of their common drefs, the natives of Norfolk Sound have a peculiar kind of cloaks to defend them from inclement weather. They appear to confift of reeds fewed clofely together.

The encouragement we met with here, with refpect to trade, was not to be complained of. We purchafed no lefs than
two

two hundred prime sea otter-skins; half that number of good seals; and fine beaver tails in abundance, besides a great quantity of slips and remnants.

CHAP.

CHAP. XI.

Leave Norfolk Sound—Anchor in Port Banks—Reasons for quitting it—Find a great number of Indians, who traffic largely with us—Several other parties of Indians trade with us.—Arrive off Queen Charlotte's Islands.

HAVING a light westerly breeze on the 23d of June, we weighed at seven o'clock in the morning, and made sail. We kept along the coast, pretty near the land, that no opportunity might be lost of finding new dealers. In the afternoon about seven, we saw a fine entrance, which appeared to be a river; but the tide setting strongly out of it, we stood into a fine harbour which opened to the south-east, and anchored there at a small distance from the shore. Surprized at not seeing any human creature on so favourable a spot, a gun was fired in the evening to rouze the curiosity of the natives: none however appeared.

Captain Dixon went in the whale-boat, in search of inhabitants; but, finding none, returned about noon. In the afternoon, he went to examine a passage we had seen to the northward, and returned about ten, without having seen a single person, though he had been to the distance of ten or twelve miles. He afterwards examined some inlets

lets to the southward, but found no inhabitants or habitations, and returned. This harbour which is situated in 56 deg. 35 min. north latitude, and 135 deg. west longitude, was named Port Banks, in honour of Sir Joseph Banks.

Unwilling to continue in a place, which afforded no prospect of traffic, we weighed anchor early in the morning of the 26th. Having no wind, the ship was towed out of the bay, and about noon we got clear of the land.

About noon, on the 27th, we saw land which had the appearance of two rocky islands; on our nearer approach, there was the appearance of a fine bay, but, upon examination, no convenient anchorage could be found in it. In the morning of the 28th, we had a fresh breeze from the west, but the weather was thick and hazy. We saw land, but, in such weather, did not choose to stand close in with it. About four in the afternoon, it ceased to be hazy, and we had a good view of the land; and observed an opening, like a deep bay, at the distance of about three leagues. We steered for this bay, but were disappointed in our expectations of finding an harbour.

In the forenoon of the 30th, the winds were moderate and favourable; at noon we saw land to the north. At seven o'clock in the morning of the 1st of July, we had a fresh westerly breeze, and stretched to the south-east. About noon we saw a deep bay, bearing north-east by east. The winds, during the afternoon, were light and variable; we therefore stood to the north, determining, if possible, to make the bay in sight, supposing it probable that we should find inhabitants there.

We had light variable airs during the night, with a heavy swell from the south-west, and in the morning of the second, found ourselves unable to reach the bay: a moderate breeze afterwards sprung up at north-east, and we stood in for the land.

At seven o'clock, several canoes appeared, full of Indians, who were returning from fishing. Some of them being clad in rich beaver cloaks, we tempted them with hatchets, adzes, toes, pans, and tin kettles. After gratifying their curiosity by surveying the vessel, and expressing their astonishment at so wonderful a structure, they began to trade with us, and we purchased all their cloaks and skins. By their significant gestures

gestures we also understood that plenty of inhabitants and furs might be found on shore.

At ten we were about a mile from shore, and saw a village consisting of six or seven huts. We steered for a bay which now opened to the east. As we advanced up this bay, we saw an appearance of an excellent harbour; but about noon the tide set so strongly against us, that we could not possibly make it; we therefore hove the main top-sail to the mast, intending to traffic with the Indians.

No less than ten canoes, in which there were about an hundred and thirty people, were almost instantly about the ship, all of whom had either beaver cloaks, or some valuable skins. They were indeed so anxious about the disposal of their commodities, that there were several quarrels and contentions among them about the priority of their coming along side the vessel, and their claims of being entitled to be served first. Perhaps they were apprehensive that we had not a sufficient quantity of toes to pay for all the articles they had brought us, for hardly any thing else was taken in barter for them, and those were eagerly demanded. About three hundred and ten

beaver

beaver skins were purchased of these people in less than forty minutes. So flourishing a trade we had never before experienced.

At three we made sail, and stood out of the bay. In the morning of the 3d, several canoes approached us; but finding the Indians who were aboard them, were some of those we had dealt with the preceding day, and knowing that they had nothing worth purchasing, we gave up the thoughts of getting into our proposed harbour; thinking it probable we might procure fresh supplies of furs to the eastward. At three o'clock we stretched to the south-west.

During the afternoon of the 4th, we had a fresh northerly breeze. Seeing a bay to the eastward at three o'clock, we stood towards it: but not seeing a harbour, nor any inhabitants, we bore away to the south.

At noon on the 5th, we were about three miles distant from shore. In the afternoon we were visited by several canoes, full of Indians, who eagerly sold us a great number of good cloaks: tin kettles and brass pans were most coveted by those people, in exchange for the goods they supplied us with.

Instead

Inſtead of coming to anchor, it was thought the beſt method of promoting buſineſs to ply along the ſhore. The weather was moderate during the night, and in the morning of the 6th, our laſt viſitors returned with ſome fine ſea otter-cloaks, which we purchaſed of them. It is remarkable that theſe people were particularly careful to conceal, from their neighbours, the articles they had bartered for.

The Indians having left us, we made ſail about two o'clock, and ſtood along ſhore. Standing in for land in the morning of the 7th, we ſaw a deep bay, and ſteered directly for it; but perceiving there was neither harbour nor inhabitants, we bore away to the ſouth. At three in the afternoon, ſeveral canoes came off from ſhore. They came from a ſmall iſland, where they lived together in a large hovel. The aſcent to this iſland from the beach is very ſteep, and the other ſides are fortified with pines, &c. This kind of fortification giving it the appearance of a Hippah, we conferred on it the title of Hippah Iſland.

From ſeveral circumſtances, we drew a concluſion that the ſavages of this place, were more ferocious than the others we had met with on the coaſt: we even ſuſpected

pected them to be canibals; their hostile appearance coincided in favour of this conjecture, being strongly armed with knives and spears. They assumed, however, an appearance of gentleness and good-nature, and strongly importuned us to come on shore; where it is probable they would not only have butchered us, but we should have furnished them with a repast.

The number that we saw of these Indians was about thirty; we bought of them a great quantity of good cloaks and skins, and, seeing no other canoes approaching, we made sail about seven in the evening.

About nine o'clock in the morning of the 8th, the Indians from the Hippah Island, whom we had traded with before, came again along-side. Having sold us their prime articles before, the furs they now brought us were of little value. We purchased their whole stock; they quitted us, and we made sail.

In the night we stood off and on, intending to be near land at day light. In the morning of the 9th, five canoes came out to us, with about forty Indians, of whom we purchased some cloaks and skins. Among these people was an old man, who informed ed Captain Dixon where plenty of furs might be procured; for which the Captain rewarded him with a light-horseman's cap, which gave him the appearance of a man of some importance.

A few women, chiefly aged, accompanied these people, whose under lips were distorted, like those of the women at Port Mulgrave. One of these lip pieces were purchased with some buttons, after the woman had refused to part with it for toes, basons, or a hatchet.

In the morning of the 11th, we had a steady breeze, and stood in for land, and kept close along shore till seven o'clock in the afternoon; when, no Indians appearing, we hauled our wind to the south-west. During the night we had a gale, with heavy squalls. The weather becoming moderate the next morning, we stood towards the land. In the morning of the 13th it was hazy. About seven in the evening it grew clear, and we were attended by several Indians in their canoes. We bought of them some excellent cloaks and skins. They were about thirty four in number, and exceedingly well armed.

From this time to the 20th, the weather was

was generally foggy, with a strong northern breeze, and frequent squalls. The same Indians that we had last traded with, came to us again, and exchanged some furs of an inferior kind, for buckles, knives, and other articles.

On the night of the 20th, and part of the 21st, we had a strong breeze, with frequent squalls. On the 22d the weather was moderate and hazy. In the afternoon of the 23d, it was pretty clear. At eight o'clock we were visited by about one hundred people in eight canoes, many of whom we had seen before. They sold us some good cloaks and skins.

About one o'clock in the afternoon, we had eleven canoes about us, with near two hundred persons, including women and children; but this was a visit of curiosity, not of business, for they brought nothing with them but a few gleanings.

Not expecting any more trade on this side of the islands that were near us, Captain Dixon proposed standing round the point. At noon the rocky point bore north 27 deg. west, about three miles distant. It is situated in 51 deg. 56· min. north latitude.

tude. The land, off which thefe rocks lay, we called Cape St. James's, this being St. James's Day.

About noon on the 27th, about thirty Indians came in canoes, and in the afternoon eighteen more; and we purchafed fome excellent fkins from each of thefe parties. In the forenoon of the 28th, feveral canoes came along-fide us, and fold us fome indifferent furs.

The weather, on the morning of the 29th, was moderate and cloudy: we tacked occafionally, in order to ftand well in with the fhore. Towards noon the weather cleared up. We were now convinced, from obfervation, that the land we had been coafting along, almoft a month, was a group of iflands.

About three o'clock in the afternoon, we were vifited by eighteen canoes, in which were about two hundred people, of whom we purchafed a vaft quantity of excellent furs: we had fo brifk a trade, that we were all fully employed for a confiderable time. Among thefe we recognized the old man, who had been complimented by Captain Dixon with a light-horfeman's cap. Finding him to be a chief of the firft confequence, consequence, the captain permitted him to come on board. He began immediately to relate a long story, of his having lost his cap in battle, and displayed the wounds he had received in defending his property; he therefore requested another cap, which he promised he would not part with but with life. The captain gave him another, for which he was extremely thankful.

On our requesting to be informed, by the old man, whether any furs were to be had eastward, to which the captain pointed, he informed us that he was always at war with that nation; that he had killed many of the inhabitants, and at that time possessed several of their heads. We were desirous of knowing how they disposed of their enemies which were slain in battle, but the chief was not sufficiently intelligible upon that subject; but there is strong circumstantial evidence that the slain are feasted on by the conquerors: they preserve the heads as perpetual trophies of victory. The old chief had that ferocity of aspect and disposition, which seemed to qualify him for a leader of a tribe of canibals.

In the afternoon of the 30th of July, a few indifferent skins were bought of a parcel of Indians, who came along side us in eight canoes: some of them had caught a great quantity of halibut, which we gladly purchased of them.

Those who sold the halibut, loitered a long time about the ship, and some of them slily paddled round her; one in particular, observing some furs piled against the cabin window, thrust his spear through it, with intent to steal them; but, finding we were alarmed by the noise, they all instantly paddled away. To deter them from future attempts of this kind, several muskets were fired after them.

Very little more trade being expected, and the time being almost arrived, which was fixed on for our joining the King George, at Nootka Sound, Captain Dixon determined to proceed thither with all convenient expedition. Early in the forenoon of the thirty-first, we stood to the south-east. During the afternoon and night, we had pretty fine weather, and light airs. On the first of August at noon we saw Cape St. James's, which bore south five degrees east. In the evening fourteen people came along-side in a canoe, not to dispose of any thing, but to inform us that one of their companions had been shot dead by one of the musket balls

which

which had been fired at them. They strove to make us understand that they harboured no resentment against us, and came only to acquaint us with the circumstance that had happened.

CHAP.

CHAP. XII.

Observations on Queen Charlotte's Islands—Meet two vessels, called the Prince of Wales, and the Princess Royal, from London—Persons, manners, and customs of the inhabitants—Dress—Manufactures.

HAVING quitted the islands, a few observations on them and their inhabitants may not be thought improper. From the number of inlets we met with, in coasting along the shore, and from our seeing the same inhabitants on the opposite side of the coast, it is more than probable that this is not one continued land, but forms a group of islands. In consequence of which they were distinguished by the name of Queen Charlotte's Islands. They are situated from 51 deg. 42 min. to 54 deg. 24 min. north latitude; and from 130 deg. to 133 deg. 30 min. west longitude.

The great quantity of furs we met with here, renders it probable that these people have no intercourse with any civilized nation; and we have reason to flatter ourselves with having the honour of adding these islands to the geography of this country. We saw but few ornaments among the inhabitants, and their knives were probably

bably acquired by war, all the tribes seeming to be hostile to each other.

The women indiscriminately distort the under lip, like those at Norfolk Sound. Though these Indians were, in general, jealous of their women, and seldom permitted them to come on board our vessel, yet some of them not only permitted, but even persuaded them, to accept of the invitations of our people; but their sole inducement was that of plunder: these tribes were the most expert and rapacious thieves of any we had met with.

We had now purchased at these islands upwards of eighteen hundred sea otter-skins, many of which were extremely fine, besides various other furs: toes were principally demanded in barter for these goods, but our dealers were so numerous, that we found it necessary to exhibit many other articles to please them all.

But to return: At noon on the 5th, we were only twelve miles north of King George's Sound. In the afternoon at six, we saw Woody Point, about four leagues distant. At ten in the morning of the 7th, we had a light breeze, and the land about two leagues distant. At ten we beheld a
sail

sail to the south-east, accompanied by a smaller vessel. Willing to be informed of their destination, or to what country they belonged, the captain gave orders to tack, and fire a gun to leeward. The signal was immediately answered by the smaller vessel, which hoisted our company's colours. They spoke us soon after twelve, and we had the satisfaction of being informed, that they were fitted out by our owners from London. The ship's name was the Prince of Wales, Captain Collinett; and that of the sloop, the Princess Royal, Captain Duncan.

These vessels, which left England in September 1786, had settled a factory at Staten's Island, to collect oil and seal skins, and had proceeded from thence to King George's Sound, without touching any where. They had been almost a month in King George's Sound, but had traded very little; a ship called the Imperial Eagle, Captain Berkeley, having got there before them.

The information we received from these vessels, convinced us that no advantage could be expected by our making King George's Sound; and they were informed by us, that at Prince William's Sound, their

next

next deftination, no encouragement could be expected.

The two captains, and another gentleman from on board the Prince of Wales, came on board us, where they continued all night; and in the morning of the 9th, we parted company, faluting our brother traders with three hearty cheers.

As we are finally quitting the American coaft, it may not be impertinent to obferve, that, though we have made fome difcoveries on this coaft, in addition to what have been already made, yet fo imperfectly is it at prefent known, that it is even doubted whether we have yet feen the main land. That the coaft abounds with iflands is certain, but whether any of the land we have been near is really the continent, future navigators muft determine.

The animals of this country may be known by the fkins we purchafed, and we have feen dogs among the natives: though they appear to be of the wolf kind, they are docile, and perfectly obedient.

The people are, in general, ftraight, well proportioned, and of the middle ftature; but thin and lean: they have alfo fmall eyes,

eyes, and prominent cheek bones. Should thefe Indians wafh their faces, their complexions would be but little darker than thofe of the Europeans. The hair of thefe people is long and black, and is capable of being rendered very ornamental, but they rub into it fuch quantities of greafe and red oker, as to make it appear extremely difgufting, though it by that means becomes a fafer afylum for the vermin. Some of the women, however, keep their hair in decent order, and tye it in a kind of club on the neck.

They have not much variety in their drefs. The coats of the men confift of fkins, made in various forms, but frequently in the fhape of a waggoner's frock; and fome of them have a piece of fur faftened round the waift. The women wear an under garment of fine tanned leather, extending from the neck almoft to the ancle. Over this is tied round the waift a kind of apron of the fame materials. Their upper covering refembles that which the men wear, and is alfo compofed of tanned leather. They refufe to wear furs, and their reafons for it fhew that they are not totally without delicacy. Should their garments be worth purchafing, which would certainly be the cafe if they were cloathed in valuable furs,

their

their husbands would strip them at a moment's warning, whenever they could find a purchaser for them.

The Indians are much delighted with masks, and caps of various kinds, which are decorated with the painted figures of beasts, birds, fishes, &c. Some of their carvings in wood have been shewn us, that were not destitute of merit.

In their singing, they are extremely exact in beating time, either with their hands or paddles; and to assist their vocal exertions, the chief shakes a kind of rattle with great glee, and accompanies his instrument with ridiculous grimaces and gesticulations.

These Indians manufacture a kind of blanket, composed of the wool or hair of beasts; they are variegated, and appear not to be woven, but to be formed entirely by the hand; they are, however, very neat, and not a little prized among them.

Exclusive of their common habits, they have large war-coats, made of the elk-skin, tanned and doubled. For weapons they have spears fixed to a long pole, and a short dagger, usually sheathed in leather, and tied round the body.

Dried fish is their principal winter food, though in their hunting seasons, they have great variety; but broiled seal affords them the most luxurious repast.

Barbarous and uncultivated as these poor creatures are, they are not ignorant of gaming. One of them, at Port Mulgrave, lost a knife and several toes, in a very short time, at a game played with fifty-two small pieces of wood, marked in different places with red paint. Though we could not comprehend the principle of the game, we observed that the excellence of it consisted in a judicious arrangement of the several sticks or men.

Having thus given a sketch of the manners of the inhabitants on this dreary coast, I shall resume my narrative.

From the 9th to the 12th of August, we had a fresh breeze at north-west; and from that time to the 15th, alternately calms and light variable winds. On the 16th we had a fresh breeze from north north-west.

In the morning of the second of September, we steered due west, in order to make Owyhee, which we saw early in the morning of the 5th, bearing from south south-west.

west. Having but a light breeze, we could not fetch the land by day light.

In the morning of the 6th, we bore to the east; and seeing several canoes at a distance, we hove to, that we might traffic with them, and bought hogs and potatoes of them in great plenty.

About eleven o'clock we were attended by a great number of canoes, some of whom were so impatient to be served, that they even climbed up the side of the ship. One in particular, seeing we were too much engaged to notice him, took a poker from the armourer's forge, and jumped over-board with it in his hand. Vain were our threats and entreaties to prevail on him to bring it back; the fellow swam off with his booty, and seemed to think himself very fortunate. He was soon after taken up by one of the canoes, but while it was making for shore, several muskets were fired at the thief, and we perceived that he had received a wound, the lower part of his face appearing very bloody. His companions, fearing they might experience the same kind of treatment, brought him along-side, and he was taken on board. His under jaw being wounded, our surgeon dressed it, and the fellow was permitted to depart; but he first

petitioned

petitioned for a toe, and his requeſt was granted.

About noon we ſaw Mowee at twelve leagues diſtant. Having moderate weather on the 7th, we plied occaſionally, that the people might bring us hogs and vegetables, with which we were abundantly ſupplied.

At three o'clock in the afternoon, of the 8th, we made ſail and bore up for Whahoo, meaning to wood and water in that iſland. In the evening of the 9th, we had ſome heavy ſqualls, but the weather grew moderate about eleven; and early in the morning of the 10th, we ſet ſail, Whahoo being right a-head, and anchored in the bay where our ſituation had been before, at eleven o'clock. This birth, however, not being ſo eligible as we could wiſh, we meant only to lay there till we could get ſupplied with wood and water.

Towards the afternoon we had a number of female viſitants, who were in expectation of getting huſbands for the night. The prieſt, of whom we have already made mention, attended as uſual, to pay his reſpects to us in the morning of the 11th, and to acquaint us, that the king intended

us

us a vifit, before the natives would be permitted to fupply our wants.

Teereteere, attended by his nephew Myaro and many other chiefs, came on board about one in the afternoon. He brought with him a hog and fome cocoa-nuts as a prefent. After making enquiries refpecting the health of Captain Portlock, and accepting of fome toes and other articles, he went on fhore, and we foon experienced the effects of his influence. We had afterwards fo many water-bearers in our fervice, that we had filled above a dozen butts before the evening. In the morning of the 12th, our remaining empty cafks were prefently filled.

Thefe induftrious Indians were then informed that we required their fervice in procuring wood: a hint was fufficient; away they paddled for the fhore, and began brifkly to furnifh us with that neceffary article. By four in the afternoon we had a fufficient quantity.

The king came a fecond time on board in the afternoon, and brought a prefent of two hogs and fome cocoa-nuts. He was highly gratified by a patou, which Captain Dixon ordered the armourer to make for him.

CHAP.

CHAP. XIII.

Teereteere comes on board to take leave—Proceed to Atoui. —Liberal behaviour of the king and chiefs. Manners, and customs of the Sandwich Islanders.

AT four o'clock in the morning of the 13th, we weighed anchor, and, with a fresh breeze, made sail for Atoui. Seeing the king putting off, we backed the main-topsail, and he came on board. He expressed his concern at our sudden departure, but took care to give us a hint of the services he had rendered us, in causing us to be so expeditiously supplied with wood and water. Captain Dixon perfectly understood his meaning, and gave him some saws and axes, with which he seemed highly pleased.

He continued on board till about eleven o'clock, when being near Whititte Bay, his place of residence, he left us, with many professions of friendship and respect. In the afternoon we had close sultry weather, and variable winds: in the morning of the 14th we had a moderate breeze; and at eight o'clock in the morning of the 15th, we saw King's Mount, Atoui, distant about nine leagues.

By

By nine o'clock in the morning of the 16th, we were within three miles of the eaſt ſide of Atoui; when ſeveral of the natives came along-ſide us, and brought us ſome taro and potatoes. We kept ſtanding along ſhore for Waymoa Bay, the wind being light and variable. Several canoes viſited us, and many of the inhabitants expreſſed great ſatisfaction at ſeeing us again. Much enquiry was made reſpecting our commodore, and many of the people expreſſed their concern that he was not with us.

We received information that Captain Meares had been at Atoui, in the Nootka, and had left it about twenty days; and that he had uſed the inhabitants extremely ill.

Tyheira, the ſon of Abbenooa, came on board, and confirmed the truth of this intelligence. The captain ſaid no traffic ſhould be permitted till Abbenooe had been on board. Tyheira ſent immediately for his father, and hoiſted a ſignal to inform him that he might ſafely venture. He ſoon appeared, and was rejoiced to ſee us, and we were equally happy to behold our old friend.

In the morning of the 17th a multitude of canoes surrounded us, filled with hogs, and variety of vegetables. Of hogs we procured as many as we wanted.

On the 18th we had a great number of visitors on board: and, among the rest, Tyheira introduced his wife and sons: the eldest was a fine little fellow, about four or five years of age; the other was an infant in its mother's arms. The woman was a pleasing figure, and had a modest diffidence about her that was engaging. Tyheira, to shew his respect for our commanders, has given his eldest son the name of Portlock, (which at Atoui is pronounced *Po Pote*) and the youngest one that of Dixon, called there *Ditteana*.

Tiara the king, about eleven in the forenoon, made his appearance in a large double canoe, and his daughter and two nieces in another. The retinue upon this occasion was numerous, and on their coming on board joined in a song that was really pleasing and harmonious. The king, when we informed him that we should only stay till we had procured a supply of provisions, expressed a willingness to see us accommodated with what we wanted. The chiefs, in general, were inclined

clined to render us any service in their power. One of them, whom we named Longshanks, gave us convincing proofs that he was not void of sensibility.

Seeing our carpenter, who appeared emaciated and pale, from having been long ill, he wept, and tenderly asked him what was his complaint. He endeavoured to console him, and gently chafed the sinews and muscles of his legs; then calling his canoe, he jumped into it, and hurried on shore, without uttering a syllable. He returned soon after, bringing with him a fine fowl, which he gave to the poor carpenter, begging him to have it dressed immediately, and he hoped it would soon make him better.

Having near eighty live hogs on board, the captain said he should speedily be in want of vegetables, as those animals would require to be fed as well as themselves. This intimation was sufficient: the king and chiefs went on shore, and about four o'clock returned, each having a canoe laden with sugar-cane and taro. Thus were we instantaneously furnished with an ample supply of every article we wanted.

Some return ought certainly to be made for so much kindness. The king was gratified with a pahou, a kind of baize cloak edged with ribbon, and a large toe: neither were the other chiefs suffered to go unrewarded. The ladies on board were also liberally decorated with beads and buttons.

Hogs and dogs were the only quadrupeds we saw in the Sandwich Islands: the dogs are somewhat of the cur-kind.

The inhabitants of these islands are, in their dispositions, inoffensive, friendly, and sprightly; they are also diligent, perservering, and strong in their attachments. It is certain, however, that they are much addicted to theft; and that they hardly look upon it a crime, for they never appear to shew any signs of remorse or shame, when they are detected in their pilfering. But let it be remembered, that if any thing is committed to their charge, they always faithfully restore it.

They are about the middle size, well proportioned, straight and slender; though many of the arees are corpulent, having, perhaps, too little exercise, and too much food. Nut-brown is the general colour of their complexion, but some of the women are

much

much fairer, and their hands and fingers small and delicate.

The people of both sexes go naked except about the waist. The men wear what is called a marrow, which is a narrow piece of cloth barely sufficient to answer the purpose for which they seem to have intended it. The women's dress, called the ahou, is much larger, extending from the waist to the middle of the thigh. Sometimes the women wear a wreath of flowers about the head; and, instead of a bracelet, a shell fastened round the wrist: but the most becoming ornament they wear, is a kind of necklace, formed from the beautiful variegated feathers of the humming-bird.

The men have caps and cloaks that are extremely elegant, particularly the latter: the ground of them is net-work, on which feathers are sewed in alternate squares, or triangular forms of red and yellow. They have really a most splendid appearance.

Mats are made by these people with great ingenuity: some of them are equal in neatness to any European manufacture. Cloth, which is made from the Chinese paper mulberry tree, is neat and elegant, and the patterns beautiful. Fans and fly-flaps are used

used both by the men and women; the former is made from the fibres of the cocoa-nut; the latter are of various kinds.

Fish-hooks, contrived with so much ingenuity as to serve for both hook and bait, are made of the pearl oystershell. They also make excellent fishing tackle of other kinds, nets, &c.

Many of their huts, or houses, resemble a stack of hay. The aperture serving for a door place, must be crept into, it is so extremely low; and the covering consists of rushes. The apartment within is usually kept neat and clean, and the floor covered with a kind of mat. Having but one room, that part of it on which the inhabitants take their repose, is somewhat elevated, and covered with a finer sort of mats. The household and culinary utensils, which are placed on a wooden bench, consists principally of wooden bowls and dishes, and a few gourds.

Their bowls and dishes are made of wood resembling ebony, and are finished and polished very neatly.

In their songs, or heevas, they attend more to the gesticulations of the body, than
the

the management and modulations of the voice. The women are the beft performers in their amufements of this kind. They are very flow and regular in the beginning of a fong, fomewhat like the Englifh Quakers in their preaching; but they gradually become quicker and more fpirited, and towards the conclufion are very rapid, and affect immoderate laughter.

Their implements of war are flings, fpears, and bows and arrows. In the ufe of flings, they are amazingly expert. Their fpears are five or fix feet in length, made of a hard brown wood, and barbed at one end. They have a kind of drums to affift in their concerts, about ten or twelve inches in height, with holes in the fides, and a hog's fkin ftrained over the top of it.

Their bodies are tatooed, but this practice is not fo general among the women as the other fex; fome of whom have had that operation performed in a very curious manner. In their falutations, they join their nofes together, and this ceremony is confidered as a token of friendfhip and efteem. Both the men and women are expert fwimmers.

They have an idea of a Supreme Being,
or

or Beings, and in the worship of their Gods are regulated by their priests; who also direct their ceremonies at funerals. The horrid custom of human sacrifices is certainly adopted by these Indians, notwithstanding their dispositions are humane and friendly. They certainly make much nearer approaches to civilization, than the miserable inhabitants with whom we traded on the dreary coast of America.

CHAP XIV.

Leave Atoui—Proceed for China—Pass the Islands of Tinian, Aguigan, and Saypan—Anchor in Macao Roads—Leave Macao—Arrive at Wampo—Difficulties occasioned by the supercargoes there.

WE weighed anchor in the afternoon of the 18th of September, and made sail. Soon after we had cleared Wymoa Bay, our friends on board took affectionate leave of us, and got into their canoes. China was our next place of destination. We had a steady easterly breeze during the 19th, and part of the 20th, but in the night we had squalls and rain. From the 21st to the 25th, we had a fresh breeze from the east.

We had not much variety from the 25th to the 8th of October, when the weather grew immoderately hot, attended with lightning and heavy squalls. In the night of the 12th, we had two very violent squalls, attended with much thunder, lightning, and rain.

From that time to the 20th, we had cloudy weather, and a steady easterly breeze. At eleven in the morning of the 22d, we saw land, and great numbers of genats flying near it. About noon we saw two islands,

islands, and, when we drew near land, we beheld three islands, which we supposed to be Tinian, Aguigan, and Saypan. These islands are so free from rocks and shoals, that vessels may safely run by them in the night with moderate weather. Tinian is the largest, Saypan the next in dimensions, and Aguinan the smallest.

We had not much variety till the 31st, when a great swell set in from east northeast, and we had heavy squalls and rain. On the 1st of November we had a moderate breeze, and at night a strong gale, which continued during the whole of the 2d. On the morning of the 3d, the weather grew moderate.

At two o'clock on the 14th, we saw a small island to the north, and afterwards another behind it. We found these islands to be Botel Tobago, Xima. In the morning of the 7th, we saw land, bearing northwest, about five leagues distant. At three o'clock in the afternoon, we past six Chinese fishing boats, and a great many more about four. At five we saw Pedro Blanco, a large rock, distant about ten miles.

In the morning of the 8th we saw the Lema Islands. At eleven o'clock, we made signal a signal for one of the fishermen to approach. Soon afterwards an old Chinaman came on board as a pilot, and produced certificates from several captains whom he had taken to Macao. After some debate, we agreed with him to conduct us thither for thirty dollars. About midnight we came to anchor in Macao Roads in seven fathom water.

As soon as it was day light, we saw a ship at anchor at the distance of about three miles. We hoisted colours, and she shewed English ones in return. At nine o'clock, the captain went on shore at Macao, to procure a choppe, or custom-house permit, for our passage to Canton, and to obtain some other necessary information.

In the evening of the 10th, a Chinese boat came along-side, bringing a gentleman on board. He informed us that his name was Folger, that he had been chief mate of the Imperial Eagle; but, in consequence of a misunderstanding between Captain Berkley, the commander of that vessel, and himself, he had left him. He then pointed to the ship we had before seen in the roads, informing us that she was the Royal Eagle. He added, that he had seen Cap-

tain Dixon at Macao, and had his permiſ-
ſion to ſail with him to Canton.

Mr. Folger informed us, that the Imperial Eagle had been no farther to the north
than King George's Sound, and that they
had procured about ſeven hundred prime
ſkins, beſides inferior ſorts. He alſo told
us, that Captain Berkley often ſent his
long-boat, with his ſecond mate, and about
a dozen of his men, to traffic with the
Indians, where the ſhip had not acceſs; and
that, upon one of theſe occaſions, the ſecond mate, accompanied by three others,
quitted the boat, and went on ſhore, taking
ſome of their commodities with them to
barter for what they could get; but neither
of them returned. Several of the ſhip's
company landed at the ſame place the next
day, and found ſome remnants of their cloaths
mangled and bloody; whence they could
not but conclude, that the unfortunate people had been butchered, and perhaps eaten.

In the forenoon of the 11th, Captain
Dixon returned from Macao, bringing a
pilot with him to conduct the veſſel to
Canton. Having the tide in our favour, we
weighed at about two o'clock in the afternoon, and made ſail, our deſtination being
to Wampo. In the afternoon about five,
we

we passed the Bocca Tygris, a narrow passage defended by a kind of fort. Soon after we came to anchor, and a mandarine boat brought a man on board, who, like an officer of the customs in England, came to prevent any illicit trade.

Early in the morning of the 15th, we made sail, and anchored at the bottom of Wampo Roads, at seven in the morning of the 16th. About eleven the captain went to Canton in a passage-boat, having first given directions for the vessel to proceed to the end of the fleet. At twelve we began to warp up the river, and came to anchor in that spot.

On the 23d we received the agreeable intelligence, that the King George was arrived at Macao; and at noon on the 25th, she came into the river, and anchored near us, her people being full of health and spirits.

Captain Portlock's success on the coast, after our separation, had been far short of that which we had experienced, but the long-boat had made a successful trading-voyage up Cook's River.

In the morning of the second of December,

ber, we were visited by the superintendant of the customs (by the Chinese called John Tuck) attended by a numerous retinue. He pretended to measure the ship, and then demanded, it is said, a thousand pounds as a port charge.

Captain Dixon went to Canton on the 4th, to prepare every thing at our factory for depositing the furs, and to engage a boat to carry them up. On the 5th a choppa came for our cargo. Accordingly we sent our whole cargo of furs of the two vessels; and when they were landed at our factory, a particular account of them was taken by a set of merchants belonging to the customs, who give security to the emperor for the duty being paid. Another account was taken by persons employed by Mr. Browne, president of the supercargoes.

After an assortment, the quantity fixed on to be sold by Mr. Browne was 2552 sea otter-skins, 434 cub, and 34 fox-skins. The remainder were to be disposed of by our captains as well as they could: they consisted of 1080 beaver tails, sundry pieces of skins and cloaks, sixty cloaks of the earless marmot, and some other inconsiderable articles.

We

We applied to a company of wealthy merchants, called Hong-merchants, to purchaſe all our furs; not knowing, that the moment they looked them over, and fixed a value on them, no other perſon durſt interfere; and, as they could not then be divided, no other perſons were perhaps able to pay for ſo large a quantity immediately.

However, on the 26th of January, 1788, our principal furs were ſold and delivered to the Eaſt India Company's ſupercargoes, for 50,000 dollars; and thoſe which we diſpoſed of ourſelves produced as follows: The 1080 tails ſold for two dollars each, the fur ſeals for five dollars each, and fifty dollars were given for the rubbiſh. One reaſon for our cargo's producing ſo ſmall a ſum was, that the merchants here had been glutted with furs.

The ſupercargoes having engaged our veſſels for the Eaſt India Company, to convey tea, &c. to England, our goods were properly ſtowed, our water taken in, and every neceſſary proviſion made for the voyage; by the 5th of February we unmoored at eleven o'clock in the morning, having a breeze at north north-weſt, and came to at three

three in the afternoon, at the bottom of the fleet. The King George unmoored in the morning of the oth, and came up with us about four. The wind being contrary, we came to every tide, and anchored in Macao Roads in the morning of the ninth.

CHAP. XV.

Leave Wampo.—Anchor in the Roads of North Island.— A dangerous storm.—proceed to St. Helena—procure water there, and some fresh beef—Arrive off Dover.

TO attempt to give a new description of China, a place so much frequented by Englishmen, so universally known, and so often described already, both by ancient and modern writers, would be adding to the bulk of our performance, without increasing its utility.

About noon on the 9th of February, we weighed anchor and stood down Macao Roads, having light baffling winds. The tide being done at half past seven, we came to. At five in the morning of the 10th, we weighed, and at ten the Peak of the Grand Ladrone bore north-east, seven leagues distant.

From the 10th to the 17th we had variable weather; and from the 17th to the 20th we had fine weather and a steady breeze. In the morning of the 20th, we saw the island Pulo Sapata, bearing south-west.

On the 25th, we saw the Anambas, a range of islands; and soon after a small island called Pulo Domar. At six in the afternoon of the 26th, we saw the island Panfang, bearing north-west, about six leagues distant. In the night we had very heavy lightning in all quarters.

On the 27th the island Dominis bore south east, and at ten at night we brought to. At five in the morning of the 28th, we made sail; and about eleven died, much lamented by the ship's company, Mr. Lauder, our surgeon.

About one we saw a range of islands extending from south to east. On the 29th, we performed the solemn office of committing the body of Mr. Lauder to the deep. He was the first person we had lost in our voyage.

At four we saw the Sumatra shore, and came to anchor at seven, in twelve fathom water. During the night, the lightning was remarkably fierce. We weighed early in the morning of the first of March, and had squally weather, with thunder, lightning, and rain: the afternoon was still more squally, accompanied with very heavy thunder, fierce lightning, and heavy rain.

At five o'clock on the 3d, we saw the island Lusa Para, which bore north-east, distant about seven miles. Having cleared the straights of Banca, we stood on during the night. From the 3d to the 6th, we had light winds and intervening calms; the weather close and sultry. In the afternoon of the 7th, the Sisters bore south-west. On the 12th in the forenoon we passed the Sisters, two small islands which we had seen ever since the 7th.

We saw North Island a-head, where we intended to take in water, early in the morning of the 13th,; but, having a calm, and the tide against us, we anchored opposite that island. By four o'clock on the 13th, being pretty well into the roads, we came to in nine fathom water, mooring the vessel with large kedge and stream cable, North Island bearing north-east, above two miles distant. Three Dutch vessels lay at that time in the roads.

On the 14th, we sent the long-boat on shore for water; and by noon on the 15th, our water-casks were filled: in the afternoon on that day, parties were dispatched from both ships to cut wood in North Island, and at six they returned with a sufficient stock of fuel. North Island is about two miles in circumference, covered with trees of various kinds, cloathed eternally with verdure, and is therefore an excellent asylum for the feathered race. The inhabitants of Sumatra are Malays, and many of them inhabit this part of the island, to get emoluments from wrecks or vessels in distress, as well as to trade with the vessels which anchor here.

From one of the Malay boats, which came along-side us, we bought some turtle. These people also deal in fowls, plantains, arrack, Geneva, &c. Having taken in a sufficient quantity of wood and water, we unmoored in the morning of the 16th, and with a fresh breeze at west north-west, made for the Straights of Sunda. About eleven o'clock, we had heavy squalls and rain. During the afternoon, the weather was moderate; but in the night we had several squalls, accompanied with thunder, lightning, and rain.

Having a moderate breeze, we made sail in the morning of the 17th, and saw the Peak of Cracatoa about noon. From that time to the 21st, we made but little progress in the Straights. In the nights we generally had squalls, rain, thunder, and lightning.

In

In the morning of the 22d, the Peak of Cracatoa bore weft by fouth, about four miles diftant; and the weather being fine and calm, we hoifted the jolly-boat, and men were fent on fhore to fill three puncheons with water. There are but few inhabitants on the ifland of Cracatoa, and thofe feem to be Malays. Like Sumatra, this ifland produces turtles, fowls, cocoa-nuts, &c.

At five o'clock in the morning of the 24th, we weighed and made fail, with a frefh breeze. At ten in the evening we anchored in forty fathom water, Prince Ifland bearing fouth. We made fail at five in the morning of the 25th. In the forenoon of the 26th, we endeavoured to work through the paffage between Prince's Ifland and Java Head. At fix in the evening, Java Head bore eaft by north, diftant ten leagues. During the night we had fqualls and rain, and in the morning of the 27th, a frefh northerly breeze.

In the morning of the 28th of March, the weather being clear and fine, Captain Dixon went on board the King George, and, on his return in the evening, acquainted us that the two veffels were to feparate, each to make her quickeft paffage to St. Helena,

Helena. In the forenoon of the 1st of April, we lost sight of the King George, and, from that day to the ninth, had a fresh easterly breeze, with some squalls and rain.

In the evening of the 16th, we had a great deal of lightning, and in the night a heavy squall; but the weather grew moderate towards the morning. We had not much variety till the 24th, when the ship's company were put to an allowance of two quarts of water per day for each man.

From the 24th, to the 4th of May, no particular occurrence happened: we then saw vast quantities of bonetta about the ship, threw out lines with tolerable success, and regaled ourselves with the fresh provision we had thus obtained. In the afternoon of the 7th, we had a fresh wind from the east, and during the former part of the night, heavy squalls, with thunder, lightning, and rain. About two o'clock the next morning, a most violent squall took us, on which we handed the topsails, and fortunately received no damage: but the weather grew moderate by day-light.

About six in the evening of the 15th, the wind blew a strong gale at north-west, on which we close-reefed the topsails, reefed the

the mainsail, and sent down the top gallant yards: the gale still increasing, at three o'clock in the morning of the 16th, we reefed the foresail and handed the topsails; the gale still continuing with great violence, and frequent heavy squalls. At four in the afternoon the pumps were choaked up. Though the ship's company were now at an allowance of water, the weather was too stormy to have it served out, and every man supplied himself with what he wanted. Still the gale continued with unremitting violence; at six in the morning of the 16th, the mainsail sheet gave way, and the sail blew instantly to pieces. The gale continued with equal violence during the afternoon, the ship laboured hard and made a great deal of water; every exertion was therefore required to keep the pump-well cleared.

Our people had, till now, been in three watches; but this tempestuous weather, and the choaking up of our pumps, requiring the strictest attention, the ship's company was put to watch and watch. During the night the gale abated, and the weather became moderate about six o'clock in the morning of the 18th. At eight o'clock a leak was found under the counter, in consequence of which several useless

less articles which had been stowed in the run, were hove overboard.

We had a fresh gale, with frequent squalls, on the 19th; close attendance was still required on the pump. In the afternoon our powder was found loose and damaged, and four barrels of it were thrown overboard. In the afternoon of the 20th, the wind shifted to the east, and then to the south, growing light as it came from the south. In the evening of the 21st, the wind blew very hard, with frequent squalls, but grew moderate in the morning of the 22d. About ten o'clock on the 23d, we had a most violent squall; but fortunately received no other damage than that of having our fore stay-sail split.

The weather being moderate and pretty well settled on the 25th, the ship's company were put to their former allowance of water. In the evening of the 27th, it blew a heavy gale, and continued with increasing violence during the night, attended with lightning, rain, and heavy squalls. Nothing particular happened from this time to the 18th of June, when we stood for St. Helena with a fresh south easterly breeze, and fine weather: at four in the morning, that island bore north-west, about six leagues

leagues diftant; the whale boat went on fhore with difpatches for the governor. We came to anchor at eleven o'clock in eighteen fathom water, where we had the pleafure of finding the King George.

Captain Portlock, in doubling the Cape of Good Hope, by keeping nearer the land than we had done, and not having fo much bad weather, had arrived at St. Helena fix days before us.

Our principal bufinefs at this ifland was to fill up our water; no time was therefore loft in furnifhing ourfelves with a fufficient quantity of that article. We were alfo defirous of procuring fuch refrefhments as the ifland would afford: but, as a great number of fhips touch here, frefh provifions are parted with very fparingly; we could only obtain three quarters of frefh beef.

We unmoored at four o'clock in the afternoon of the 24th, and made fail, having clear weather and a light eafterly breeze. About eleven on the 25th, Jamestown bore fouth-eaft, ten leagues diftant. Our paffage from St. Helena to Dover produced nothing particularly remarkable; and we arrived off the laft mentioned place on the 17th of September, where we had the pleaſure to be informed that Captain Portlock had been moored in the Thames about fourteen days, his ſhip's company being all in perfect health.

THE END.

INDEX

A

Abbenoue, Chief 57, 59, 62, 121
Aguigan Island 130
Ahou (women's dress) 125
America 8
Anombos Islands 138
Arms of War 127
A Tappo village...........60, 61
Attoui (Hawaii)..........23, 24, 39, 52, 58, 64, 65, 120, 121, 129
Ava (drink) 47

B

Banks, Sir Joseph............98
Bay Islands 34, 36
Bears 29, 32
Beauty, Native 87-88
Beavers 96, 100, 101, 134
Bengal, India 76
[Beresford]-Dixon (cf. Dixon) ...V
Berkeley, Capt. 112, 131, 132
Berries, wild 94
Blankets, native............115
Bocca Tygris 133
Bonavista 6
Bonetta fish 142
Botel Tobago, Xima Island ...130
British Museum V
Browne, Mr. 134
Burials (Alaska)............89
Burning Mountain 28

C

Canary Islands 6
Cannibals 103, 107, 132
Canton, China.....131, 132, 134
Cape Bede..................32
Cape Edgecombe 34, 91
Cape of Good Hope.........150
Cape St. James..........106, 108
Carcase Island 15
Caskets 4
China 1, 129
Christmas-day 53
Claret 5
C.L. (author) ....III, V, X
Clothes, native 95, 99, 114-115, 125
Cloth (Hawaiian)............125
Coal Harbour 26
Cocoa-nuts......52, 62, 119, 141
Codiac Indians (Kodiak).......26
Codiac Island 76
Collinett 112
Cook, Capt. James........IX, 20, 21, 40, 41, 47, 52, 68, 69, 75
Cooking, Alaskan 89
Cook's River 24, 26, 37, 76, 80, 94, 133
Cracatoa Peak 140, 141
Cross Sound 33-34, 36

D

Dances (Hawaiian) 127
Deal.......................2
Discovery (ship) 75
Dixon, [Beresford] Capt. ......V, VI, X, 2, 5, 20, 22, 31, 44, 54, 59, 73, 74, 76, 77, 78, 84, 85, 86, 93, 97, 104, 105, 106, 108, 119, 120, 122, 132, 134, 141
Dolphins 39
Dominis Island 138
Dover, Eng.................150
Downs 2
Ducks................16, 72, 87
Duncan, Capt. 112

E

East Hummock 42
East India Company 135
Eddystone 13
England 16, 58, 59, 95
Ermine 32

F

Falkland Island 15
Ferro 6
Fish 83, 116
Fish tackle 126
Folger, Mate 131, 132
Foot Island 69
Foxes (skins) 32, 37, 134
France 4
Fur trade 1

G

Gaming 116
Geese 16, 72, 87
Grand Ladrone Peak 137
Gravesend 1, 2
Green Island 72
Guernsey 4
Gulls 72

H

Halibut 108
Hayley, Mrs. 14
Hayward and Hill 80
Hinchinbroke Cove (Cape) 73, 74, 84
Hippah Island 102, 103
Hogs 44-45, 49, 50, 52, 53, 58, 59, 62, 117, 118, 119, 122, 123
Hong-merchants 135
Humming-bird 53
Hussey, Capt. 14
Huts, Alaskan 88
Huts, (Hawaiian) 126

I

Imperial Eagle (ship) 112, 131, 132

J

Jamestown 150
Java Head 141
Jones, Inigo 88

K

Karakkakooa Bay (Hawaii) 19, 20, 40
Kay's Island 84
Kempenfeldt, Adm. 3
Keppel's Island 15
King George (ship) 1, 20, 25, 51, 52, 55, 73, 77, 80, 81, 82, 84, 108, 133, 136, 141, 142, 150
King George's Sound 80, 111, 112, 132
King's Mount. Atoui 120

L

Lauder, ship's surgeon 138
Lei 125
Lema Islands 130
London 8, 14, 112
Longshanks, Chief 123
Lufa Para Island 139

M

Macao, China 131, 132, 133, 136
Madeira 6, 7
Malaya 140, 141
Margate 2
Marmots 29, 32, 37, 86, 134
Masks 115
Meares, Capt. John 76, 77, 78, 81, 121

Meteor 37
Monakeah, Mt. 39
Montague Island 33, 69, 72, 73, 74, 84
Morotoy (Hawaii) 42
Mount St. Elias 84, 93
Mount Senis (Savoy) 39
Mowee (Maui) 40, 41, 118
Musquash 32
Myaro, Chief 44, 119

N

Nankeens 26
Nootka (ship) 76, 77, 78
Nootka Sound 35, 36, 70, 108, 121
Norfolk, Duke of 94
Norfolk Sound 94, 97, 111
North Island 139
Nose-rubbing 127
Notooneshuc (otter skins) 70

O

Oneehow (Hawaii) 23, 51, 55
Oonalaska 26, 76
Oruhoura Island 64
Otter skins 37, 74
Owhyhee (Hawaii) 19, 20, 22, 39, 40, 41, 42, 65, 116

P

Pacific Ocean . . . . IX, 20
Palma 6
Pansang Island 138
Patagonians V
Pedro Blanco 130
Penguins 16
Pennant, Mr. 38, 53
Piapia, Chief 44, 51, 58
Pilfering (cf. thieving) 82
Port Banks 98
Port Egmont 13, 14

Port-Egmont hen 16
Portlock, Captain . . . . . . V, VI, X, 1, 2, 7, 13, 24, 27, 30, 51, 55, 57, 67, 77, 81, 82, 119, 122, 133, 150, 151
Port Mulgrave 86, 91, 94, 104
Porto Santo 6
Port Praya Bay 6, 7, 8
Portugal 4, 9
Portuguese 6, 8, 9
Priest (Hawaiian) 47-48, 49, 50, 118, 128
Prince Island 141
Prince of Wales (ship) 112, 113
Princess Royal (ship) 112
Prince William Sound 33, 36, 69, 70, 72, 76, 78, 80, 84, 85, 86, 94, 112
Puffins 67
Pulo Domar Island 138
Pulo Sapata Island 137

Q

Queen Charlotte Islands 110
Queen Charlotte (ship) 1, 5, 14, 73, 77, 80, 82

R

Racoons 29, 32, 37
Royal Eagle (ship) 131
Royal George (ship) 3, 5
Russians 25, 26, 31, 71, 76

S

St. George's Sound 34
St. Helena Island 3, 141, 144, 150
St. Hermogenes Island 24
St. Jago 6, 10, 18
St. James Day 106
Salmon 27, 29, 30
Sand-piper 38

Sandwich Islands 19, 20,
  23, 35, 39, 78, 124
Saypan Island 130
Sea-lion 68
Sea-otters (cf. otters) 29,
  85, 86, 93, 96, 99, 102, 111,
  132, 134
Seals 11, 96, 135
Sharks 17, 38, 47
Silks, Persian 26
Sisters Islands 139
Snug-Corner Cove 74
Spain 4
Spaniard 17
Spithead 3
Stanway, Chief 81, 82, 83
Staten's Island 16, 112
States Bay, Swan Island 15
Straights of Banca 139
Straights of Sunda 140
Sugar-cane 52
Sumatra Island 138, 140
Supreme Being 127
Swan Island 15

T

Taro 52, 60, 62, 65, 121
Tatoos 44, 127
Teereteere, King 43-44, 46,
  49, 59, 119
Thames River 151
Thieving 82, 94,
  111, 117, 124
Tiara, King 59, 66, 122
Tinian Island 130
Toes 100, 111, 116,
  119, 124
Tuck, John 134
Turtles 18, 140

Tyheira, Chief's son 57, 61,
  62, 121, 122

U

United States (ship) 14
Utensils 126

V

Vegetables 59, 71, 79,
  122, 123
Vinegar 10, 11

W

Water 94, 119, 139,
  140, 142, 143, 150
Wampo Roads, China 132,
  133, 137
West-point Harbour 15
Whahoo (Oahu) 22,
  42, 51, 54, 118
Whales 11, 24, 84
Whitsuntide Bay 76
Whititte Bay 120
Whitworth, J. V
Wolves 32
Wood 54, 71,
  79, 94, 118, 119, 140
Woody Point 111
Wymoa-Bay, Attoui 23, 51,
  57, 64, 66, 121, 129

Y

Yam-Bay, Oneehow 23, 55, 63
Yams 55, 64
Young, James V

COLOPHON

The William Colin Lauder (presumably) A VOYAGE ROUND THE WORLD IN THE YEARS 1785, 1786, 1787, AND 1788, *was printed in the workshop of Glen Adams, which is located in the sleepy country village of Fairfield, southern Spokane County, Washington State. It is an enlarged facsimile of the rare 1789 London edition plus limited added prelim material, plus an index by Edward J. Kowrach. The index was not in the original edition. The added material was set by Sharyn Brown using a Model 7300 Editwriter computer photosetter. The title page is set in several sizes of Baskerville Bold with other new material in Baskerville Roman and Italic. Camera-darkroom work was by Evelyn Foote Clausen. The film was stripped by Dale LaTendresse. Plates were made by Tami K. Van Wyk. The sheets were printed by Robert LaTendresse using as 28 inch Heidelberg press, model KORS. Folding is by Garry Adams using a 22x28 three stage Baum folding machine. Assembly work was by Millie Ferger and Tami K. Van Wyk. The paper stock is 20 pound Hammermill cream white. Binding is by Willem Bosch of Oakesdale, Washington assisted by Gerit Bosch, Bill Harnois and Dorothy Dineen, who sewed the books on a National book sewing machine. The gold foil stamping of the cases was done by Willem Bosch, Jr. This was a fun project. We had no special difficulty with the work.*